A word about t...
Toastmasters

Who needs another book on public speaking, let alone a series of them? After all, this is a skill best learned by practice and "just doing it," you say.

But if practice is the best solution to public speaking excellence, why is this world so full of speakers who can't speak effectively? Consider politicians, business executives, sales professionals, teachers, trainers, clerics, and even "professional" speakers who often fail to reach their audiences because they make elementary mistakes, such as speaking too fast or too long, failing to prepare adequately, and forgetting to consider their audiences.

As we experience in Toastmasters Clubs, practice and feedback are important and play major roles in developing your speaking skills. But insight and tips from people who have already been where you are might help ease some bumps along the road, reinforce some basic public speaking techniques, and provide guidance on handling special speech problems and situations you may encounter. The purpose of *The Essence of Public Speaking Series* is to help you prepare for the unexpected, warn you of the pitfalls, and help you ensure that the message you want to give is indeed the same one the audience hears.

This series features the accumulated wisdom of experts in various speech-related fields. The books are written by trained professionals who have spent decades writing and delivering speeches and training others. The series covers the spectrum of speaking, including writing, using humor, customizing particular topics for various audiences, and incorporating technology into presentations.

Whether you are an inexperienced or seasoned public speaker, *The Essence of Public Speaking Series* belongs on your bookshelf because no matter how good you are, there is always room for improvement. The books are your key to becoming a more effective speaker. Do you have the self-discipline to put into practice the techniques and advice offered in them?

I honestly believe that every person who truly wants to become a confident and eloquent public speaker can become one. Success or failure depends on attitude. There is no such thing as a "hopeless case." If you want to enhance your personal and professional progress, I urge you to become a better public speaker by doing two things:

- Read these books.
- Get on your feet and practice what you've learned.

Terrence J. McCann
Executive Director, Toastmasters International

"It's nice to find a book on speaking that goes beyond the 'how to's' to unleash the authentic power of a strong purpose and a passion for message. This is a MUST READ for any speaker who wants to speak from the inside out."

— *Terry Paulson*, PhD, professional speaker on
Making Change Work and 1998–1999 President,
National Speakers Association

"If you speak to 1 or 1,000, Shirley Nice gives you practical ideas and a step-by-step guide to cut years off your learning curve. Speaking for Impact *can get you more fame, fortune, and success, but you do have to read the book!"*

— *Patricia Fripp*, CPAE, Speaker, Author, Past President
National Speakers Association

"What a great book! I enjoyed it from the first to the last paragraph. It's a confidence builder, strong and to the point. We may not all be public speakers but we all communicate with each other and this book makes it easier. It's a winner!"

— *Bruce Ramm Andresen*, Director, MAIN REMIX
INTERNATIONAL, LTD.

"This book offers great insight and tangible advice to speakers. Beyond mechanics, she has captured the more important preparation required for credibility and impact— in a unique and readable book, structured for both novice and experienced readers."

— *Sandy Cook*, Manager, Global Consulting Practices and
Human Resources, Hewitt Associates

"Reading this book is to experience total re-evaluation: overcoming my fears, finding my own source of passion, and getting it across to others. I found it especially helpful for developing briefings when I'm under pressure to get my ideas accepted. This book is not just for professional

speakers and trainers, but for everyone who needs to communicate ideas clearly and get a response."

—*Diana Dravnieks Apple*, Strategic Planner, U.S. Forest Service, Washington, DC, and former National Secretary, Phi Beta Kappa Associations

"So beautiful, energizing! Wise, witty and practical. It's not just about speaking but about writing, all artistic expression, about life!"

— *Rita Cashman*, Corporate and Business Coach, Cashman & Associates

"Shirley Nice is breaking new ground in Speaking for Impact. *This very readable book is both a reference for all professional speakers as well as a tool for teaching others the art of public speaking. This goes on my 'A' list."*

— *Willie Jones*, Toastmasters International 1997 World Champion of Public Speaking

"Speaking for Impact *is filled with genuine Golden Gems—a wealth of wisdom generously shared by 14 top caliber presenters. The value of tips included will shave years off platform trial-and-error, ideal for any level of presenter. Shirley Nice has balanced the heart factor with delivery and content, offering a Gold Mine!"*

— *Sheryl L. Roush*, DTM, Toastmasters International Accredited Speaker, International Speaker/Trainer/Author, President, Creative Communications

"This book targets the often neglected aspect in the communication process, the audience. Fine tuning to each audience is especially critical in the international arena and Shirley's book shows you how to get it right."

— *Elizabeth Urech*, International Consultant, Speak for Yourself, Zurich, Switzerland

SPEAKING FOR IMPACT

Connecting with Every Audience

SHIRLEY E. NICE

WILLIAM D. THOMPSON
Series Editor

ALLYN AND BACON

Boston   London   Toronto   Sydney   Tokyo   Singapore

Printed in the United States of America
10 9 8 7 6 5 4 3 2 1   02 01 00 99 98

Contents

Foreword ix
Preface xi

PART I/ Meeting the Impact Imperative

CHAPTER 1   What Do Today's Audiences Demand?   1

PART II/ Getting in Touch with Your Own Impact

CHAPTER 2   Open a Window to Yourself!   24
CHAPTER 3   What Do You Bring to the Party?   36
CHAPTER 4   What Is Your Message? Finding a
Simple Dwelling in the Center of a
Complex World   50
CHAPTER 5   Where Is Your Passion?   60

PART III/ Finding the Impact Fit with Every Audience

CHAPTER 6   What Audiences Hear and Remember   84
CHAPTER 7   The Four Faces in Every Audience:
Finding the Fit with Diverse
Audiences   98

PART IV/ Mastering the Three Essentials for Impact

CHAPTER 8   The Speaker Makes It Safe   115
CHAPTER 9   The Speaker Defines the Space   134
CHAPTER 10   The Speaker Lights the Energy   153

Foreword

This is a personal book. It comes from 30 years of professional experience in the field of interpersonal communication: radio, theater, high school and university teaching, television, corporate training, executive coaching, and, of course, public speaking. I've drawn from all phases of my expertise as a speaker, actor, director, producer, professor, trainer, mediator, and coach.

- Over 1,000 presentations to audiences worldwide.
- Fifteen years as a management skills trainer to corporate and small business clients and to federal, state, and local governments.
- Ten years consulting with the banking industry.
- Fifteen years as a professional mediator.
- Twenty-five years as extension faculty with the University of California, Berkeley.
- Visiting professor at University of California, Los Angeles, Santa Cruz, and Davis; Texas Tech University; and the University of Southern California.
- Master's degree from Northwestern University in Speech Communications.

This book is an integration, a collage that interweaves information, personal experience, and practical relevance with conversation, humor and reflection. I trust you will enjoy the book as much as I have loved writing it. Within these pages, I hope you find exactly what you need.

Shirley Nice

Preface

The trumpets signal,
The house darkens.
A spotlight circles an actor
on the stage
of England's Chichester theater.
Sir Lawrence Olivier stands quietly,
His eyes encompass the audience.

Now, years later,
I can still feel that moment.
A man on a stage,
Speaking beyond words,
Speaking to me.
Impact!

This book is written to everyone who has ever felt a special connection across the footlights, at an inspirational meeting, in the classroom, or with someone in your life. It's written to every person who has ever wanted to make an impact, to be better understood, to step out a little from the crowd and contribute something special. Though aimed specifically to speakers, the wisdom and the information of this book translates to every person who searches for better-quality human connections.

Uniquely personal, it integrates the professional experiences of a 30-year veteran speaker with the advice, tips, and techniques of 14 additional professionals. It's written in a conversational style about real people, using real names and experiences. It will take you to a new perspective with audiences, one you'll not find in other speech texts. Combining facts with possibilities, specific situations with practical applications, it is graphic, earthy, visual, and humorous as it speaks to everyone who has ever stood before an audience.

The book is also a metaphor for integrating the diverse learning styles, taught in its four parts—an integration each speaker must master:

Part I—presents the "big picture" of what audience's demand of speakers today.

Part II—puts the spotlight on you and how to find your unique impact potential.

Part III—gives you the data, the facts, and the concepts about how to work with diverse audiences.

Part IV—integrates specific situations with tips and techniques about how to connect for impact.

It is the author's confidence that, when you finish reading, you will be able to:

■ Define your own uniqueness and message.
■ Feel more confident with diverse audiences.
■ Avoid the blunders with audiences that come from "not knowing."
■ Take a step closer to having an impact on all people.

At the very least, this book will be a good read, and it just might change your life.

ACKNOWLEDGMENTS

I want to thank Dr. Bill Thompson for the opportunity to write this book and for his wise suggestions and encouragement. I also want to thank Dylan Kelling for the drawings and for his enthusiastic support of this project.

To the professional speakers who so freely volunteered their wisdom and experience, and to those who allowed me to practice some of the techniques on them, how can I thank you enough?

K. C. Chan, M.B.A., of the Geneva Consulting Group, San Francisco, California

Rita Derbas, of Rita Derbas Speaks, Newark, California

Patricia Fripp, CSP, CPAE, Cavett Award Winner, San Francisco, California

David Garfinkel, of Overnight Marketing, San Francisco, California

Frederick Gilbert, Ph.D, of Powerspeaking, Redwood City, California

Jennifer Esperante Gunter, of Gunter Productions, Santa Rosa, California

Arlene Kaiser, of Arlene Kaiser Productions, Milpitas, California

Allen Klein, CSP, of Award-Winning Presentations, San Francisco, California

Annette Martin, of Honolulu, Hawaii

Marianna Nunes, of Burlingame, California

Karen O'Brien, of VSI, Inc., San Francisco, CA

Jim Prost, of San Francisco, California

Padi Selwyn, of Sebastopol, California

Bob Treadway, CSP, of Treadway & Associates, Inc., Walnut Creek, California

1 WHAT DO TODAY'S AUDIENCES DEMAND?

Where better to go
Than to the speakers,
The professionals
Who are out there doing it!
Ask them:
What do their audiences demand?

We're sitting together at the Connections Cafe, a room set aside for coffee and networking at a Saturday morning meeting of the Northern California National Speakers Association. It's an informal time when speakers share ideas and swap information with colleagues, and I'm here with my tape recorder to talk to speakers about their take on the question,

"What do today's audiences demand of a speaker?"

Patricia Fripp, one of the nation's busiest and most accomplished speakers is first. "I believe that what audiences want is *wisdom* from the speaker's point of view. If you've written a book, draw from your absolute bottom line keys of wisdom. If you haven't written a book, take the wisdom from your life. In a 45-minute keynote speech, it's not knowledge but wisdom from your point of view that's important. What audiences want is something they can't get anywhere else!"

Rick Gilbert, founder of Powerspeaking, a training ground for business speakers, pulls no punches. Known for down-to-earth candor, Rick fires from the hip: "I think audiences want *sex* and *money.* If you look at the books and speeches that really sell, they fit into two categories: (1) How am I going to become richer, more successful, more powerful, more in control? and (2) How do I get love, how do I lose my fat thighs? . . . I think this is about 90 percent of the whole deal. People aren't craving enlightenment, I think it's about money and sex." And then, as if hearing himself on a roll, the real catalyst hits him: "I'll tell you what audiences really *don't* want—to be bored! When the guy gets up there and starts reading his overhead slides, it's finished!"

K. C. Chan, who speaks internationally to corporate audiences, adds a third dimension. "My audiences want to know how to feel comfortable working with people from different cultures. They want *content* that they can hear at 11:00 A.M. and be using by 1:00 P.M. They want suggestions, techniques, and statistics they can immediately apply."

Jennifer Esperante Gunter, 28-year-old dynamo in the youth market, joins the conversation. Jennifer talks to kids, her e-mail address is ChaQueen, and she's hot! "I'll tell you," she says, "bottom line, what my audiences want from me is that I'm fun, entertaining, and exciting enough that they think I'm worth listening to. They don't want content but if I mask the content in entertainment, they'll absorb it. They want to be entertained."

Arlene Kaiser, who is wearing her trademark unmatched shoes, is next. Never at a loss for words, this wonderful woman with the broad smile defines her audience, "I talk to teachers, counselors, and school support staff like bus drivers, cooks, and maintenance workers. And I'll tell you, they want to be *inspired* and *motivated.* They want simple strategies they can use on the job and in their teaching. They will say they want guidance on handling the new curriculum, but when I give them a simple message that reaches their heart, they walk away with an 'Ahaa.' They never get enough acknowledgment; they get the head stuff, but they hunger from the heart."

We snag **Bob Treadway,** one of the leading platform authorities on the future. "Audiences want information *customized* to their specific situation; that's an ongoing demand. The days of having a canned speech and maybe changing a word or two with some added references are gone. In order to continue to have a market place, 15 to 20 percent minimum of a presentation needs to relate specifically to the audience."

David Garfinkel, a marketing expert who speaks on "The Secrets of Direct Mail Marketing," interjects a word of caution: "I think people feel burned by a lot of the advice they've received in the past, suggestions that sounded good but didn't really make things better. With so much pressure to produce profits and with competition so fierce, customers are looking for a bargain, but when that bargain doesn't produce anything they feel cheated. They want their money's worth, which means *results that work."*

Padi Selwyn joins the conversation. Her background is Madison Avenue, banking, and media; she speaks on "Creativity and Life Balance" as she balances a busy career with kids and husband. "Padi, does your market demand experts?" Her answer, "Yes, more than ever before! *Expertise* is real-life experience that can offer something new."

Rita Derbas picks up on Padi's contribution: "I speak to a lot of high-tech companies, and my audiences want *new perspectives.* They want to know how they can do things in a different way when they're going through change. They say to me, 'We're not in denial, we're not in resistance, we're in just plain chaos.' They're looking for speakers who understand their industry and their issues."

As a final comment **Allen Klein,** a humor educator, summed up his experience: "My audiences demand something that will improve their lives. On some level, they want to know how they can *make things better."*

Ten professional speakers, ten different types of audiences, and ten pieces of the big picture of what audiences want: As we listen to both speakers and audiences, five demands flesh out the fuller picture!

THE DEMANDS OF TODAY'S AUDIENCE

1. Connect with Us!
   - Get and hold our attention!
   - Entertain us.
   - Talk to us personally!
2. Don't Hype Us, Be Credible!
   - Be an expert.
   - Don't waste our time.
   - Have something important to say.
3. Customize to Us!
   - Know our industry.
   - Speak our language.
4. Give Us Substance!
   - Say something we can use immediately.
   - Say something new.
   - Give us answers, solutions, tips.
5. Make an Impact!
   - Give us something to remember.
   - Make our lives better.

Let's look more closely at each of these demands and read what the professional speakers have to say from their own experiences.

1. Connect with Us!

- Get and hold our attention!
- Entertain us.
- Talk to us personally!

Today, the need for connection is so great that people walk around with pagers talking into cell phones. While technology keeps us talking, there's a deeper connection that people need and that's a more meaningful connection with themselves. Disconnected by routine jobs, derailed careers, forced retirements, and loss of meaning—audiences look to speakers to reconnect them.

Inwardly, speakers ask:	Audiences respond back:
■ How do I get through to them?	■ Help us solve our problems.
■ How do I touch just what they need?	■ Give us something that will get us through.
■ How do I make a difference for them?	■ Make some meaning out of this.

For speakers, this challenge of connecting becomes even more complex as diversity increases. We are performers, entertainers, teachers, and leaders. We're trend setters, change agents, conflict managers, and peace makers. We're students, business leaders, service providers, community activists, doctors, lawyers, researchers, counselors, technical and financial experts, athletes, parents, and retirees. We are members of service organizations, focus groups, professional associations, church fellowships, and educational and community groups.

We speak from platforms, in meeting rooms, in conference centers, in churches and community halls, at association

meetings, and at professional study groups. We talk before
large audiences and small informal gatherings, to all kinds of
people, from the formally educated to those raised in the
school of hard knocks, from kids to seniors, the interested
and the disinterested. We speak across ethnic and cultural
borders, with interpreters, and in all countries. We encounter
special interests, the angry and the disenfranchised, the
lethargic, and the comfortable. Today's audiences are a sexual,
cultural, linguistic, color mix of multiple backgrounds and
varied experiences. The challenge for us is to connect with
this array, helping them build connections both with each
other and the larger world.

> **Arlene Kaiser,** education market: What I do is present
> the bigger picture to my market. I help teachers make
> the connection between the outside world and what
> they are teaching. Wherever I go, I ask questions like
> the one I asked Steve Wosniak of Apple Computers,
> "What is the most important thing I should be teach-
> ing kids in the classroom; what most impacts the work-
> force?" He said, "Teach your students to be helpful to
> each other." I connect teachers to these truths.

A speaker is like a rubber band that has to stretch around
a whole bunch of odd shapes and yet retain its own form. To
over-stretch, is to break. To stay in the stretch without returning to our own significance is to lose our elasticity. Our challenge is to connect with every audience from the integrity of
who we are and the reality of our own experience. Impact
begins when we release ourselves from the yoke of *having* to
make an impact!

> **Patricia Fripp,** speaker to all markets: You need to be able
> to present your wisdom in a sound bite, because today's

audiences are stimulation junkies with short attention spans. I use statements that I call "Frippicisisms," bumper-sticker statements like "Your business is as good as your worst employee," and "Think big, start small." Audiences connect with these and remember them.

Rick Gilbert, business speech trainer: We asked a cross section of our business audiences "What is wrong with business presentations today?" Out of 250 responses, 44 percent targeted *style:* boring delivery, not reaching the audience. We say, get really good with your delivery, be sure your message is clear, and then handle the environment correctly. Audiences want to be stimulated; you can laugh or cry or intellectually stretch them with new ideas; whatever, people don't want to be bored!

Marianna Nunes, corporate market: You know, I do a topic called "Leadership 10l: God Grant Me Patience." Personally, I would never pick that title; a client picked it. But I come in on a motorcycle! You know, they're most excited about the motorcycle; I don't even think they care about the content, it's the motorcycle!

Jennifer Esperante Gunter, youth market: In my first ten minutes, I give a lot of high entertainment so they think, OK, she's worth listening to, and they sit back and keep their ears and hearts open. Kids have short attention spans. The younger the age, the shorter the span. My major audience is high school age. Since they watch a lot of TV at night, the usual sitcom is about a seven-minute segment and then a commercial, then another seven-minute segment. So, I figure their attention span with me is about seven minutes. What I do is get their attention, put in some content, tell a story, and then break the content by doing something that is fun and exciting. Then, another seven minutes with some content and stories and another switch. This keeps them with me, even after a whole hour.

Padi Selwyn, creativity and marketing: I can remember before I was a professional speaker and knew better, coming back from a business talk I had given and saying, "I had such a boring audience this morning. They just sat there!" I look back now, and I'm embarrassed that it came out of my mouth. Excuse me! Who was boring? Whose responsibility is it? I was so arrogant that I blamed a flat speech on the audience.

One of the strongest and most poignant examples of an audience crying for connection is the picture of the British people grieving over the tragic death of Princess Diana. This was the drama of a princess who connected with her audience in a new way, daring to step out of tradition and let herself be seen. It's the drama of a national audience who saw themselves in her reflection and were also able to break tradition and express themselves openly. Connected in grief, they were able to put aside party lines and search for a redefinition of dignity and courage. And it's the drama of a world audience that found themselves so personally connected that for days, all watched in stunned silence.

In a shrinking world, the demand for connection is all powerful! It is the first door a speaker must open on the path to impact!

2. Don't Hype Us, Be Credible

- Be an expert.
- Don't waste our time.
- Have something important to say.

Some people are good bluffers who thrive on their ability to walk into unfamiliar situations and ace them. This can be a great skill for getting in the door, but today's audiences want specialized experience, and if you do manage to con your way in, you had better be a fast learner. Unless you're a master of one-night stands with no returns and no paper trails, speak only on topics where you have credibility. The standard for this credibility is both audience perception and proof of experience. Do some careful thinking about: (1) how you want to be perceived; (2) what credibility you want communicated; (3) how to communicate your expertise in an effective yet comfortable manner.

How Do You Want To Be Perceived?
How do you want the audience to see you?

- As a teacher, a seminar leader, a trainer, or an educator?
- As a speaker, a storyteller, a problem buster, or a consultant?
- As a "global citizen," "snake lady," "Mr. Vitality," "Hungarian dynamo," or the like?

> **Arlene Kaiser,** education market: Often when my introduction is read, I see eyes rolling back, I hear sighs and see the back row taking out papers to grade because they think, "Here comes somebody who hasn't a clue as to what's going on in the classroom." Then, when I say, "I had to get a substitute for my classroom in order to be here," it's like the scales drop from their eyes, and I get back, "You speak our language."

Are you in touch with your full offering, your uniqueness, expertise, and message? Begin a list of everything you bring to an audience. Live with your list, add, combine, and prioritize. Come to know the essential strengths that you offer and the perception you want every audience to get!

What Credibility Do You Want Communicated?

Allen Klein, humor educator: I think one thing that
gives me credibility is that I tell personal stories, and
audiences see me as a real person. I don't have the
words perfect all the time and I don't always have the
answers. Recently, I was conferencing with a client who
told me all the problems of his company and I had to
say, "You know, I'm just going to be with you for an
hour; I can't answer everything. What's most important?" I want to be known for that kind of honesty.

K. C. Chan, international/corporate market: Sometimes a
person goes overseas for a couple of years and comes
back and wants to be an international speaker. It's
really important that you have the expertise to back
you up. I would be insane talking to my market if I had
not worked in the corporate world. One of the bench-
marks is that you have to have enough experience to
help you understand a particular market.

What credibility do you lead with? Have you written a
book on the subject? Do you have years of experience in the
field? Maybe it's simply that you've been there!

Rick Gilbert, business speech trainer: People want to
hear from those who have actually done it, been there!
They'll pick the astronaut over Rick Gilbert, and pay
tons to hear him speak, even if he's a poor speaker,
because he's been there! Take Captain O'Grady, the guy
who was shot down in Bosnia. He was just a guy who
flies an airplane and believes in the free enterprise system. He's shot down, he's a little bit articulate, they give

him some intensive coaching, and he's possibly making $30 thousand a pop. Of course it's temporary, he's got a shelf life of six months, but he's the guy who did it!

No matter what you write in promotional brochures, your credibility begins with how you see yourself and your contribution to the audience.

- ▪ *Be who you really are.* Make sure the weight and quality of your experience match your self-promotion. Know who you are before the makeover, before the shave and the face lift! The closer you can be to that person, the stronger your impact.
- ▪ *Keep it simple.* It's less confusing and definitely less stressful. This way you don't run the danger of falling out of character.

How Do You Communicate Your Credibility?

Tooting your own horn can be uncomfortable. Having someone toot it for you can be a risk. Well-intended introducers can cut into your content, destroy your opening moment, and even present the wrong information on you. Realize that everything the audience sees and hears about you moves to your credibility. Give consideration to doing the following:

- ▪ Write out the script for your introducer to either read or memorize.
- ▪ Think through, specifically, how and where you want to interject self-promotion within your speech.
- ▪ Check the look of all visual materials: handouts, overheads, flip charts, slides, and video:
  1. Does everything have the same congruent look?
  2. Have you taken every opportunity for self-promotion?
  3. Is your identification on everything?

3. Customize to Us!

■ Know our industry.
■ Speak our language.

To customize is to fit or alter to individual specifications;
whether it's filling a special order or fitting to an exact size.
Audiences expect accuracy, timeliness, big picture context,
industry specific content, and personalization.

Know Their Industry!

How much do you know about the culture, the environment, the problems, concerns, and successes of your audience? To customize to an audience means to be:

■ *Industry specific.* This is a corporate term referring to companies, associations, and businesses, but it can refer to any
audience. If you're speaking to kids, it means giving specific content about their school, their neighborhood, their
club, their home; for senior citizens it means specific stories, facts, and metaphors on their issues and challenges.
"Industry specific" means getting down to names, places,
people, and issues that directly touch your audience.
■ *Timely.* Keep current! Check the morning newspaper or
the latest professional journal for a gem that can be salted
into your talk at the last minute. Do you know something
about the audience that hasn't yet been announced to
them? The more current your information, the greater the
potential for impact.
■ *Connected to the big picture.* Your ability to accurately fit
specifics into a larger context that addresses the audience's
situation will both impress them and confirm your credibility. Audiences like to hear their own specifics strategically placed within the larger frame of their own situation.

Rita Derbas, high-tech market: My clients are looking
for a speaker who knows their industry and their issues.
They demand I translate that understanding to them.

Speak Their Language!

Today's audience looks you in the eye and says, "Talk to us!" They want you to speak *their* language, know *their* acronyms, and personalize to them.

> **Allen Klein,** humor educator: My real customization is on the spot. I put up a blank overhead and say, "OK, what is stressing you out in your industry?" Now, I know the stresses before I go in, but I want it to come from them. I want to meet their needs, so I make a list of what they identify and then I weave those needs into everything. I customize by going directly with what comes from the audience.

Can you call people by name and acknowledge individuals within your talk? A misspelled or mispronounced name can destroy the credibility of hours of preparation. Messing up on an acronym will be remembered longer than the point you are making. You must be accurate when referring to their world.

4. Give Us Substance!

- Say something we can use immediately.
- Say something new.
- Give us answers, solutions, tips.

> **Patricia Fripp,** speaker to all markets: Substance is what can make an audience's business and personal life better if they act on it.

A satisfied audience walks away with something solid in hand, a three-step strategy, a book to read, or a tip to make the job easier. Take-away value is more than a pleasant evening; it's a cash benefit to take to the bank, back to work, or to try out at home. The standard is always, "Can we use it, right now, today?"

Something New!

Bob Treadway, corporate/business market: From a corporate perspective, I think expectations are that they must have something concrete and some application. There's much less tolerance for fluff. New focus, new ideas, new ways of looking at a situation are all part of making it tangible. A lot of times speakers relabel and repackage and call it new, but audiences aren't stupid: Once it's repackaged, there has to be something in there that's new.

Padi Selwyn, creativity and marketing: I think the whole concept of adding something new is part of expertise. In one sense, there is nothing new under the sun, but the way it is presented and combined is new.

One service that the speaker renders is to provide synthesis and context, which lead to new perspectives. Though audiences want their pain acknowledged, they need help to see how their issues and problems fit the larger picture, to expand their vision, and to explore available options. This is always, always a customized piece.

Rita Derbas, high-tech market: When there is an information glut, context is needed. I think speakers provide that context! We bring a realized value to all this information.

All of the books and articles on the metaphor of chicken soup reveal a truth about soups and speakers. Every time you add a carrot or an onion to the soup, it's a new mix. Every time the speaker updates a story, customizes to an audience, or personally finds a different perspective, speech becomes new. The ingredients may be staples but it's always a fresh mix!

5. Make an Impact!

- Give us something to remember.
- Make our lives better.

> **Allen Klein,** humor educator: Audiences are demanding from speakers something that will help them improve their lives. They want to know how they can make things better, in their business and personal lives. If we don't touch their lives, we're wasting their time. Why else are they in our programs?

Impact Can Be a Collision!

The wrecking ball slams into the wall of a building and a ton of bricks falls on the unsuspecting actor: you stagger out of the movie saying, "Wow! That was great!" This is collision impact.

Speakers use a lot of collision impact. I remember negotiation expert Ed Brodow throwing a rubber chicken onto the stage floor and stomping on it! Donna Hartley begins her presentation in pitch darkness with the deafening sound of a plane crash screaming into our ears. With media images, compelling sound tracks, and a range of theatrics, speakers exalt new ways to grab audiences and catapult them to a different reality. With the endless theatrical possibilities, there's always a caution about getting caught up in a dependence on collision impact and finding yourself in an escalating loop that demands every move to be stronger, harder, and more jolting than the last. Collision impact has a definite place in the speaker's repertoire, but it can leave everyone a bit dented, desensitized, and asking for less intensity, fewer gimmicks. I think one of the challenges for speakers today is to develop unique approaches that do not compete with the pressure of acceleration but rather find new ways of connecting at even deeper levels.

Impact Can Be a Gentle Touch

There is a level of impact that does not rely on shock or effects; it's a softer, more subtle impingement that is equally compelling. It can be the irresistible draw of a personality, an encounter with one's own truth or the touch of possibility, a simple message from someone who has been there before and gives you hope. It can be the magnetic presence of a speaker or the logical clarity of an expert who has done the homework. This level of impact comes silently, often unexpectedly, and reveals itself so deftly that everything shifts.

> **Allen Klein,** humor educator: When I first got into the speaking business about 12 years ago, I had an incredible revelation. I was doing an all-day workshop on humor in 10 different cities, and in one city I had an audience that laughed every two minutes. I thought, "What a great group!" but their reviews of the workshop were not as great as I expected. The next day, the audience laughed OK and their reviews were absolutely glowing. That's when I realized that it's hard to read impact with a group, because you never know just how you touch people. It was then that I knew I was teaching something incredibly valuable.

As we speak to audiences, we say to them, "Hear us, believe us, take what we say and use it." Audiences respond, "Teach

us, see us, be special, acknowledge us, make a difference."
Speakers want to get through and make a difference. Audiences
want answers, resources, options, and personal connection.
Both want impact!

Three Levels of Impact

There are at least three levels of impact uniting speaker
and audience. Every speaker goes for at least one; great speakers go for and get all three.

First Level of Impact: The Audience Hears You!

They let you in the door, they listen to you without cutting the volume or switching channels. This first degree of
impact is an initial acceptance. When you get this, your
speech goes well, you get and hold the audience's attention,
and their feedback confirms they heard you. They accept
your credibility and are expectant about what you have to
say. With some audiences, this is your target impact.

Second Level of Impact: The Audience Gets It!

You really get through to them! Logically it registers and
emotionally it touches. They remember, they tell others what
you said, it sticks! Months, even years later, they recall in
detail. This second degree of impact is the "Ahaa!"

Patricia Fripp, speaker to all markets: Impact, to me as
a speaker, is when the audience walks away and says,
"Wow!" They might not give a standing ovation; they
may just sit there in stunned silence because what you
just said was so meaningful and profound. Most of us
don't have the confidence to know that we are a success when this happens.

Third Level of Impact: The Audience Takes Action!

They *do* something! The impact propels them to move. They revise a belief, start practicing a new skill, go home and lay out plans for a new direction, call a friend, or follow through on a procrastinated commitment. This third degree of impact is *action.*

High-impact presentations get all three A's:
Acceptance, Ahaa, Action.

THE PRESSURES TO PRODUCE

There's so much competition now for audience attention, we often find ourselves trying to be technician, promoter, and expert, as well as performer. As we grapple with the expanding stages of our speaking experience, an early key decision is choosing a topic. What topics are audiences demanding? What's hot, and what will be around for awhile?

For insight into this critical area, who would be better to talk with than futurist Bob Treadway?

What's Hot!

Treadway: The future is hot. Actually, very few people speak on the future. Many think they do, but few have the background, the continuity, and the overall big picture needed.

Nice: What does a futurist have to have?

Treadway: A speaker who deals with the future needs to have hard factual data to back up assumptions and to show audiences the reasons behind his or her conclusions. Anyone can step up in front of an audience and make predictions; a futurist is someone who says, "I will make some predictions; I could be wrong about them, but here is my basis, and I invite you to take my infor-

mation and compare it with yours and come up with
your own conclusions."

Nice: What's the difference between speaking on the
future and speaking on change?

Treadway: Change people are in the present, and the
futurist is in the big picture, which is typically out at
least one to five years. Change speakers talk about what
is staring at them right now.

Nice: How hot is change right now?

Treadway: I don't see it slacking off. An observation
though, the people who speak from a human rela-
tions/resource standpoint are going to become less and
less in demand; those who speak strategically about
change as it relates to organizations in our environment and what individuals need to be prepared will be
more in demand.

Nice: Of course, technology is hot!

Treadway: There is often a confusion here. Technology
is a standard part of the future and will accelerate, as
will presentations around changing the business environment, in terms of new skills that are currently not
even being taught: for example, the ability to communicate nonsimultaneously; how to do excellent voice
mail, effective e-mail, and how to deliver and conduct
a video conference; how to leave a video message for
someone; and how to talk to your computer.

Nice: Then there are all the hot topics that nobody can
yet forecast.

Treadway: I see more and more pragmatism, less healing of the corporate wounded. Another hot topic is
"How to Work More Effectively from Home."

Nice: What about team building?

Treadway: Team building will continue to be hot; it's the
obvious way to work on projects. Another hot topic,

"How Do You Manage Laterally" or how to manage a network of people in an environment where you do not have direct face-to-face contact. How do you manage without physical proximity?

Nice: What about motivational speakers?

Treadway: The meetings industry is not going to go away. There will always be gatherings, interacting, and rubbing shoulders. However, in those situations, people want to be uplifted and entertained; the style is not going to be the same in the future.

Nice: How will the style change?

Treadway: More and more practical, more take-home value. Motivational speakers are doing more and more work at a pragmatic level. Humorists are using more content. The trends are definitely toward higher content, usable information, and specifics in terms of examples and action.

What Do I Choose?

Somewhere in finding the balance between what's hot and what we think the audience wants to hear, there's the temptation to switch around with topics looking for an advantage. In our earlier conversation, Allen Klein spoke to me of an experienced speaker he knew who was caught up in this topic confusion. Allen recalled, "I remember talking with a colleague who's also an expert with humor, and I asked how things were going. He said, 'Well, things have kind of slowed down, I think there's too much competition in my field, I'm going to switch to diversity!'"

Rita Derbas also spoke to this same tendency: "I was at a conference where I heard a stress management expert speak on leadership. He was such a hit when he spoke on stress the year before, that he was invited back, but this time to speak on leadership. His leadership content was not half as engaging as his stress material. If he truly wanted the second engagement, he had two options: he could stretch himself to adapt the topic of leadership to his already successful style or he could say, "No, I don't speak on leadership." As speakers, we're often tempted to do what we don't do well.

To adapt your topic to an audience means to make a modification or an adjustment, not a significant alteration or a complete turnaround. To adapt means to adjust the fit of your talk so that it brings you into harmony with an audience. To adapt to audience demands means first to hear the difference between what they *want* and what they *need*.

Audiences: Wants versus Needs

■ A company says that they *want* training, but you discover they *need* to revamp their reporting system. Do you give them what they want to the exclusion of what you see they need?

Audiences want speakers to connect and customize to them, to be credible, to give substance, to personalize and entertain them, to provide impact! Filling these wants can open a door to the deeper audience needs. "Need" signifies bottom-line survival; its companion is distress. When that distress is relieved, the need may shift and become more apparent, easier to address. An audience may want vision and insight for an upcoming decision; they may need immediate release from stress or answers and techniques for improving their present situation. Want tells you about appetite, capacity, and preference; need signals urgency and necessity.

■ An audience wants an expert because they need the assurance of credibility.

■ An audience wants facts and figures because they need help in decision making.

■ An audience wants humor because they need a release from the tension of their work.

> **David Garfinkel:** One of the biggest mistakes in topic selection is that we pick what we want to talk about or what we decide the audience wants, rather than what they tell us they need.

Listen carefully for this distinction when you customize. You adapt to their wants in order to meet their needs!

Keep Your Integrity

Adapting does not mean being all things to all people, nor does it mean changing just because you think the audience wants it. It never means presenting less than your strongest self, hiding your uniqueness, relinquishing your message, or surrendering your passion. Never sacrifice this integrity.

The integrity of a document is judged by whether it's the complete original. The integrity of a premise is in its consistency, its simplicity, and its avoidance of deception. The integrity of a speaker involves all of the above to include authenticity, originality, and lack of artifice. To have integrity is to be whole, not splintered up in some desperate adaptation to reach an audience. Stay close to the trunk, not out on the limb. Never abandon yourself in order to please an audience. Unless you come from the full strength of your own integrity, you cannot hope to have an impact on that audience. You must know the boundaries between adaptation and compromise lest you become a grasshopper, jumping from topic to topic, from one adjustment to another. This means getting and staying in touch with:

- ■ Who you are.
- ■ What you have to say.
- ■ Where your passion is.
- ■ Where your body of knowledge/expertise is.
- ■ Where you are unique.

2 OPEN A WINDOW TO YOURSELF!

An open window
Invites light
Not darkness.
An opening
Welcomes what is new.
New is the discovery of *now*.

*The very act of speech is courageous because no matter what
we say, we are revealed.*

David Whyte, *The Heart Aroused*

The American playwright Arthur Miller, in his play *After the
Fall,* gives us a picture of one man's self-discovery. The play is
said to be autobiographical and written after Miller's breakup
with Marilyn Monroe; Miller's principal character, Quentin,
stands center stage questioning whether or not to begin a
new relationship. As he opens this "window to himself," all
the people from his past file noisily up the spiraling stairs
behind him, and he realizes they're all coming with him into
a new life. In a moment of decision, he accepts and integrates
his past into a new beginning.

Speaking is always a beginning. When you chair a meeting, teach a class, or give a presentation, your fears, strengths,
mistakes, and accomplishments, the whole collage come with
you into the presentation. The quality of your connection

with an audience is determined by who you are, the breath of your experience and the mastery of your skills. No amount of rehearsal or bravado can cover you up.

YOU ARE THE WINDOW

When you stand before an audience, debrief a work group, or speak face-to-face with another person, it's like you're seeing each other through a two-way window. You look through it to the audience and what you see depends on the size and condition of your window. Small, thick panes of glass that have clouded over from lack of fresh air ideas do not give you accurate feedback. The audience wants to see their own world reflected in your window. No matter how grand your exterior, if it does not reflect them, they won't see what they need. When what they see matches what you see, when your window is clear and open, it will reflect light and invite impact.

There are four sections to your window: (1) platform, (2) mask, (3) blinders, and (4) source. Each section is a part of you; each is connected to the whole and serves a unique function (see Figure 2.1).

Figure 2.1

The Speaker's Window

Platform	Blinders
Everyone sees	Others see
Mask	**Source**
You see	No one sees

Your Platform

Let your experience be a stepping stone for working in the world.

Pam Chodron,
Start Where You Are

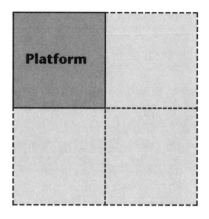

Your *platform* is the public part of you that everyone sees when you interview, consult, market, socialize, and speak. This is who you disclose through your stories, experiences, and wisdom; who you market in brochures and on the Web. You walk onto your platform with your hair combed and your day in place, and the sign in your window says, "Open for Business." This is the confident, skilled, open part of you, the available you. This is the public person you show to the world.

I've purposely chosen the word *platform* for this part of the window because it's such a powerful image in the speaking world. It has three dimensions for us:

1. *Platform connotes public visibility.* It's the stage you stand on for an audience to fully see you. It's not a private place; you don't go home, kick off your shoes, and take the platform (unless you're a little strange).

2. *Platform reveals your content and issues,* your beliefs and positions, where you're coming from. The original meaning of a keynote speaker is one who presents "the platform." Your platform is both what you stand on and what you stand for.

3. *Platform is also a verb meaning to speak out,* to take the floor, to declare a position, to make a speech. Your platform is your arena, your ground territory, both your theater and your open forum. It's your scene of action, the

marketplace where you meet and communicate. It's what you consciously present to an audience.

Some Speakers Have Large Platforms

Large-platform people converse on many subjects, comfortably meet new people, and usually are generous with their time and information. To maintain a large platform it takes a window open to fresh ideas. "What you see is what you get" is the statement of a confident platform posture. The larger your platform, the more you have to draw; the more you've done, the more you know; the more audiences you speak to, the broader your platform.

Some Speakers Have Smaller Platforms

New speakers with limited audience experience and only one or two talks under their belt may work from smaller speaking platforms. Those who lack self-confidence and feel the need for more control signal small platforms. These speakers may stay close to their scripts, lack flexibility with audiences, and find it hard to incorporate tough feedback. They are often less personally available, their public offering is usually less varied, and they do not reveal much of themselves to an audience.

High-Impact Speakers Continually Expand Their Platforms

Platform size is never fixed! Every speech, every audience, every cab ride expands your platform. Impact with an audience means exploring new information and experiences, new technologies, and new people. Resist the temptation to get comfortable because today's marketplace demands that you constantly stretch your comfort zones. Your platform expands every time you take a risk.

Your Mask

*You can't have creativeness
unless you leave behind the
bounded . . . .*

Joseph Campbell

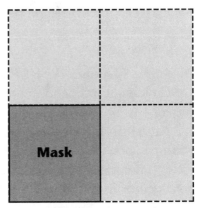

Your mask represents the
part of you that you keep
from the audience, what you
think you must conceal. Behind the airbrushed headshots
and state-of-the-art brochures is an ever-challenging list of
masks that conceal our private fears and sometimes expectations. Have you ever worn a mask to cover any of these issues
with an audience?

- You have less experience in their field than advertised.
- This is your first talk on the subject.
- You have no experience in the presentation subject area.
- The topic no longer interests you.
- You are really nervous.
- You don't want to be here.
- You no longer believe some of the material you are still
  using.
- You don't like this particular audience or person.
- You would prefer to avoid this city and especially this
  hotel.
- You get tired of hearing about people's incessant problems.
- You can't wait to be finished and out of there.
- The one negative evaluation ruined the whole evening.
- You're exhausted.

It's important to look carefully at any mask issue that you have. Generally, the more masks you wear, the less impact you will have with an audience. People have a way of knowing when you bring only a small part of yourself to them. When you leave the stage and take off the public face, an audience may well ask, "Who was that masked man?"

Before you accept that speaking assignment, before you commit to develop and customize a presentation, ask yourself, "Is my platform large enough to be open and real with this audience?" because any perceived mask will reduce impact. Re-evaluate the issues that you tend to mask; it might empower your talk to bring them onto the open platform.

The line between your *platform* and your *mask* is never fixed; it moves with each experience. The larger your mask, the smaller your platform. As you grow in experience, skill, and confidence, your platform expands, and mask issues shrink. Some questions to ask yourself are:

- ▪ Am I considering a topic area where I cannot be candid, open, and totally myself?
- ▪ Do I consider my credibility strong enough to survive openness in this area?
- ▪ Do I have enough knowledge and experience to handle the topic area or the audience with ease?
- ▪ Do I feel confident in my ability to present a high-impact speech to this audience?

A "no" answer to any one of the above questions points to a mask. When you wear a mask, you work harder and are less effective; eventually the mask wears you down. Impact depends on you letting go of the mask and bringing the issues into the light of your platform.

Your Blinders

Standing on a whale and fishing for minnows . . .

　　　　　　Joseph Campbell

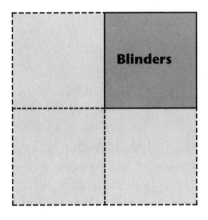

Your blinders are what you think you're concealing but everyone else sees, and what works against you that you don't see. Wearing blinders often creates those blind spots like the approaching car you can't see passing you from the rear. In the speaking business, blind spots can lead to disaster. Here are a few of them that can block speaking success.

- Feeling inadequate.
- Having negative attitudes about a specific niche market, industry, or person.
- Being resistant to a standard, a requirement, or an expectation.
- Not listening, not hearing what people say to us.
- Insisting on staying with a topic that may no longer be working for you.
- Believing we may not have a market for what we really want to say.
- Believing that we cannot be ourselves and be successful.
- Sticking to a process that's not working for us.
- Doing what other people tell us without honoring our own judgment.
- Going with what's hot instead of where our passion is.
- Having to be right.

> **Jim Prost,** marketing expert: One of the blinders that speakers wear is the perfection myth. They think they need to be perfect for the audience to like them, while

audiences really like us for our imperfections. The audience has to be able to say to the speaker, "Hey, I'm like you."

No matter how carefully you choose your topic area, impact will be reduced if you're in a blind area. Before you can handle audience feedback evaluations, or criticism, you need a realistic view of your own work, lest you tend to feel attacked, get defensive, and discard the feedback. And it is in the feedback from audiences that your blinders dissolve. I asked Jim Prost to recall a specific situation where he learned about himself from the audience.

> **Prost:** I used to see myself as a content speaker and not a motivational speaker. Since my expertise is in marketing, my strength has always been in delivering cutting-edge, high-content concepts, and information. When people from my audiences began to come to me and say things like, "You motivated me to go back and get my master's degree," or "You gave me confidence," then I began to realize I was much more than a content person.
>
> **Nice:** What did this tell you about yourself?
>
> **Prost:** That I connect with my audiences and touch their souls. I still frame myself as a high-content speaker, but now I'm more in touch with my full impact.

Farmers used to strap leather blinders over the plow horse's eyes so they wouldn't see the juicy green grass and tasty flowers growing at the edges of the furrows. Perhaps that's one of the reasons we leave our blinders on, so we're not tempted to leave our ruts!

Blinders keep us from seeing behaviors, mind sets, and fears that operate in our life. They can block the good stuff, like seeing the fuller impact of our speaking and acknowledging our talent and uniqueness.

- The blind spot blocks your impact because you don't know it's there; you can't integrate it.
- The mask blocks your impact because you know it's there and you try to hide it.

Recently, I was reading in the newspaper about black holes. They were humorously depicted as invisible black blobs flying around and splattering unannounced on the windshields of our spaceships. I thought, "What a perfect metaphor for the blind areas in our speaking!" Be on the alert for these invisible black blobs, and if one hits your windshield, make friends with it and invite it onto your platform. Blind spots are visible only when they hit us! They are the "Ahaas" of our lives when suddenly we get it!

Your Source

To create the golden moment, we must know where the gold lies in ourselves.

David Whyte,
The Heart Aroused

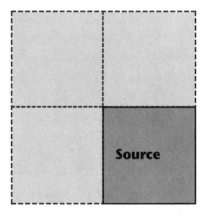

Seen neither by you nor the audience, your source is where your message and passion live. This is your private stock, your personal, inner resource, the mythological cave where your treasure is buried. It can be a dark and frightening place because it's often unknown territory. You can live a normal, well-adjusted life, even a successful one, and never explore it; but you won't be a speaker of impact. To have impact with an audience means to touch the audience at the entrance to *their* source, and you can't do that unless you've been there yourself. So, where do you start this exploration? How do you connect with your own deep pockets? Everyone finds his or her own way; I'll start with a personal example.

When I started to write this book, I literally spent weeks preparing to begin. Most of my life, I've been involved in the performance world as a teacher, radio director/producer, theater director, personal coach, corporate trainer, and speaker. So I thought, "All I need to do is a kind of cut-and-paste job with the concepts, strategies, and ideas I've worked with." Sitting in the office of my platform, I pulled out the file boxes full of materials and started writing pages of great-looking outlines. Feeling in control of my direction, I prepared for what I thought would be the finishing touches of putting it all together. The moment of truth was soon to dawn.

Where to start? A blank screen does not excite my imagination. After a few days of false starts, I went back to cranking out more outlines, hoping that somehow, magically, everything would leap up on the screen and fit together. There is a Japanese movie called, *Woman in the Dunes,* about a trapped woman who tries unsuccessfully to crawl up mountains of sand, and I felt like that woman. Every start brought data cascading down on me; and, instead of clarifying my escape route, it only obliterated what I thought was my path. I was filling pages, but my cut-and-paste job resembled a Dr. Frankenstein surgical transplant; it looked real enough, but it felt dead. I needed a body, a living energy that would breathe life into the faceless facts, theories, and strategies, and I didn't know where I had to go in order to find this aliveness. So I kept writing until finally I found my way to the entrance of *my source* and walked inside. To find the entrance, I had to do four things:

1. *Be willing to let go of old baggage.* I had to be willing to start from scratch, to set aside my props and files and start fresh. Instead of trying to fit everything in, I had to get comfortable with the blank page.

2. *Honor what I have to say.* Here I was with stacks of what other people had said, but what did I have to say? What was my message, *my* passion? Here was my entrance!

3. *Be willing to pay the price without knowing the outcome.* Outlines feel safe; going into the unknown does not guarantee coming out in alphabetical order. It's hard to escape the initial fear that maybe there's nothing down there but a lot of dark space. I had to be willing to start the journey even when I couldn't see my way.

4. *Commit to staying with the process.* Connections and discoveries emerged only when I went deep enough to find them. It was like taking the cover off an old well and starting to explore it with a very small flashlight. Staying connected to this exploration eventually brought a whole new perspective, but it took a commitment.

As you bring up your source material into the light, as blind spots come into the flashlight's beam, and as masks are lifted, your platform expands in two directions. Your speaking impact starts with clearing your blocks of stuckness, stereotyping, low expectations, mind sets, lethargy, and even comfort. Eventually, you wind up with an expanded platform and smaller masks and blinders. The only part of your window that never changes size is your *source.* No matter how much you draw from it, there is always more. You never lose it, you just forget, sometimes, where the entrance is.

WHAT DOES THIS SAY TO THE SPEAKER?

Research, preparation, and practice are all necessary; but somewhere in the process, you need to clear the deck and create an empty space. Spend time in that space, look around you, and listen; pay attention to what enters your knowing.

When you feel dead-ended, frustrated, running on empty—go to this space within you, and just be there for awhile. Take a drink from your own private reserve. It will restore, give you the answers for which you search, and ultimately direct you to the path of impact.

LOOKING AHEAD

In the next three chapters, we'll examine this path to impact. In Chapter 3, we'll look at what you bring to the speaking platform: your stories, your expertise, and your uniqueness. Chapters 4 and 5 take us to your source with your message and passion.

The Window to Yourself

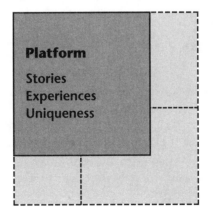

3 WHAT DO YOU BRING TO THE PARTY?

A briefcase?
Slender, compact, one size fits all.

A treasure chest!
Magical, transformational, alive!

Look carefully
Because you bring yourself.

80 percent of life is showing up!

Woody Allen

For years, Russell Maeth was a regular on my party invitation
list becaused he always brought himself fully to any party. Russell taught Chinese in Spanish to international students in
Mexico City, and his treasure chest was full of stories and experiences with unique and obscure details. An expert in his field
and an expert at recall, he could fascinate any group of guests.

When you accept a speaking engagement, do you know
what *you* bring to the party? For starters, you bring the basic
entrance fee of a well-prepared speech and probably a handout. Fine, what else? An expertise, a special knowledge, a
background of experiences, an unusual talent, a prior association? Do you bring wisdom, a good sense of humor, an ability to energize a group? Do you fully bring yourself? This

Figure 3.1

The Speaker's Platform

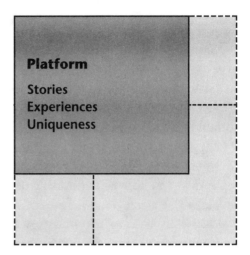

chapter is about *you*—about connecting with your treasures and reassessing their value (see Figure 3.1).

CONNECT WITH YOUR STORIES

The only story you can really tell from the platform is your own.

■ What has happened in your life that is a story?
■ Who has crossed your life that is a story?
■ What lessons and learning come from your stories?

If all the stories of your life were laid end to end, what an autobiography!! Have you traveled, written a book, raised children, run a business, built a house, learned a language, developed a Web site? Do you have a career, have there been a variety of jobs, have you lived abroad? Have you cared for an elderly parent or survived the death of a child? Have you ever been fired from a job or gone through a life-threatening experience? Have you been in love, known a time when life totally flowed, accomplished what you never believed you could? Your life is full of stories.

Start Recognizing the Stories of Your Life

I remember a small movie theater in San Francisco where everybody introduced themselves and all went for drinks together after the film. And a bus driver in Chicago who displayed a huge front window sign, "The Happy Bus," and personally welcomed everyone who boarded. I remember Mrs. Parker, a hill country woman living in the stone hut across the road from my parents' farm. She was dying of cancer. I remember my last conversation with her in that dark little house with its cement floor and bear cage built into the wall—which leads to another story about an old Norwegian man who built the stone hut for his pet bear. Stories take you to stories; don't let them get away from you.

Keep track of the little experiences; talkative cab drivers, sales clerks, chance encounters—all supply wonderful material. An overheard conversation at a restaurant, a series of small disasters that turn into an unexpected ending, these are all your stories! Everything is recyclable; every story is usable somewhere, to some audience. A great artist and good friend, Zubel Kachadoorian, once said to me as he scuffed the dirt with the toe of his shoe,

> *"The artist never complains about his materials. He creates with whatever is there."*

So does the speaker. Our materials are the experiences of our lives, no matter how ordinary or insignificant they seem. There is a magic in the treasure chest that can transform the simplest story into a connection with an audience.

Keep a Record of Your Stories

When a story happens or comes to mind, write it down, and keep a reference inventory. For example:

He said he was my neighbor in the next block and that he was looking for good homes for a litter of pups. As I told him of the family across the street whose dog had just died, I opened the front door a little wider. He casually mentioned a neighborhood girls' soccer team that was playing on Sunday and how they needed uniforms. Before I knew it, I was handing him $5.00. As I shut the door and watched him evaporate into the street, I said to myself, "I've just been conned."

I can use this story in the following contexts:

1. Handling the unexpected.
2. Reading the clues of body language.
3. Making the most of every experience.
4. Do we really listen to what we hear?

Your best speaking material comes from your stories.

CONNECT WITH YOUR EXPERTISE

Do audiences want experts? Yes! More than ever before.

John Mahr, founder of the Delancey Street Foundation, a successful alcohol and drug rehabilitation center, was once asked in a TV interview, "How do you get to be an expert?" His immediate response was,

> *"You just tell people you're the expert. If you say it often enough, people will start saying, 'Oh, yes, he's the expert!'"*

This bald statement seems to be a popular recipe for the one-minute expert of today. In this world of self-proclaimed experts we need to reexamine the basis for our own expertise: (1) Is there a standard for who is an expert? (2) Am I an expert? Let's look!

The Expert Standard

Who is an expert today?

An expert is someone who knows so much about a subject, an issue, an industry, or process that people seek his or her opinion and value it (which usually means, they pay for it!). "Expert" is not an arrival place! Information changes so fast that you can be expert today and obsolete tomorrow. "Expert" is a fast pass into the specialist pool where you have to keep swimming like crazy to stay afloat. To be an expert implies measurement against four criteria: knowledge, experience, achievement, and recognition, with some degree of mastery in all four areas. If you have:

1. *Special skill and/or knowledge,* means you have professional training and/or extensive practice in a particular field, industry, or subject area. Examples include:
   - You received the actor of the year honor with Goodman Theater in Chicago.
   - You've been doing research on the Mayan Indians for 20 years.
   - There isn't anything you don't know about that particular model.
   - You know every step of the procedure and can do it in your sleep.
2. *Substantial experience* is when you have a hands-on supremacy in a specialized area. The words *expert* and *experience* are inseparably linked; wide experience and extensive practice are requirements. Examples include:
   - You have 25 years experience in the banking industry.
   - You've repaired every model that has been put on over the last 10 years.
   - You know what it is to be poor and experience poverty.
3. *Achievement and contribution,* you deliver a new perspective, a different connection, a unique synthesis, new information, or a special emphasis. The expert goes

beyond using the work of others: You put your own contribution into the pool. Examples include:

- Allen Klein's latest book brings humor to death and dying.
- Impact is not the strength of your contact on another, it's the synergy of two connecting.

4. *Recognition and acceptance,* you have some acknowledgment by the industry, other experts, and your audiences. Examples include:

- Articles in industrial trade magazines recognize your expertise.
- Letters of acknowledgment from clients reflect your results.
- Your credentials exhibit your public and professional scope.

Are You an Expert?

These are the questions you must answer for yourself:

- How much skill and knowledge do you need before you can call yourself an expert?
- How much is *substantial* experience?
- How do you know if you have made a *special* contribution?
- How much industry acceptance does it take?

Because the market demands experts, there is always the temptation to simply promote ourselves as experts and then scramble to fill the shoes later. A starting place is to ask yourself, "Are you mainly a *content* or *process* speaker?"

Content Speakers

Content speakers are information driven. They are accurate and comprehensive with the latest updates. If you are a high content speaker, you must:

1. *Constantly upgrade.* Keep current on your subject, procedure, enterprise, company/industry, or body of information. You must know the latest trends and look ahead.
2. *Clearly communicate information.* You must be able to visually communicate an understanding of specifics, larger
   contexts, and connections. Though often billed with
   promises to educate, inspire, and entertain, your primary
   draw is that you are an informational expert in your field.
3. *Take an audience from information to knowledge.* Moving
   beyond information means connecting the information
   to the larger picture, successfully visualizing and organizing information to reach audience needs. If you are a
   dynamic content expert, you not only excite your audience members with your scope of information, but you
   enlighten them with possibilities, and leave them with a
   deeper understanding.

   Examples of content speakers are:

- The astronaut who speaks from his or her actual experiences in space.
- The CEO who returns from a conference and informs the
  audience what's happening at the top.
- The teacher who has pioneered a radical new system for
  teaching languages and overviews the latest results.
- The adventurer who scaled Mt. Everest and empowers us
  to challenge ourselves.
- The futurist who projects us ten years ahead.

Process Speakers

Process speakers are usually generalists who take their expertise across industry lines and adapt it to fit whatever organization or group they are with. They also educate, inform,
inspire, and entertain, but their major thrust is to provide
and promote a process, a way of achieving results. If you are a
successful process expert, you have three distinct skills:

1. *Translating.* You can take your process into different systems, change the appearance to fit the visual constructs, transform, remodel, and reconstruct so that people in all disciplines can "get it."
2. *Seeing the big picture.* You are skilled in seeing how everything fits into a larger framework. You give people ways to expand their own visions and apply what they know.
3. *Building connections.* You are experts at connecting concepts, meanings, and methods. You have a sixth sense that sees the gap in a situation and moves to build a connecting bridge.

Examples of process speakers are:

▪ The mediator who speaks on the process of dispute settlement and is an expert at teaching others.
▪ The negotiator who talks about the process of how to negotiate the best available deal.
▪ The facilitator who is an expert in team building.
▪ The speaker who understands the process of building self-esteem and helps others to follow it.
▪ The marketing expert who shows how to put a business on the map.

Which Are You?

Are You a Content Expert?

Is your strength in what you know, the experience you've had, your connections in the field, the books you've written, or the reputation you've acquired? When you stand before a group, is it your knowledge and experience that showcases you? Is your basic goal to inform people, to leave them with specific content, to increase their knowledge base? Are you a speaker who has been there, done it, and can give a first-hand account? Does your persuasion, inspiration, and information come from this expert base?

Are You a Process Expert?

Is your strength in facilitation, reducing conflict, helping people cope with competitive environments, increasing sales, or improving customer service? Are you confident that you can improve an audience's situation or meet the needs for which you have been hired? Is your primary attention given to focusing content for specific results?

Which Is Your Perspective?

Because of the demand for high content today, sometimes we assume that we all have to be content experts. Beginning speakers can overwhelm an audience by packing too much content into a speech. Process speakers often market themselves in terms of their content without realizing the subtle but powerful distinction in perspective.

Do you . . .

- Give workshops on how to handle difficult people, or are you an expert at building connection?
- Speak on self-esteem or show people how to find and capitalize on their strengths?
- Talk on diversity or help organizations to more fully utilize their employees?

Process expert Alan Weiss, in a taped interview for the National Speakers Association, told an audience, "I hate the question, 'what do you speak on?' What I do is I help improve the client's condition."

Ask Yourself These Questions

1. Where do you see yourself right now, content or process?
   a. Are you information based?
   b. Are you method, action, and result based?
   c. Are you a mix of both? If so, which is predominant?

2. Do your skills fit the above assessment?
   a. Content base: Information expert, cutting-edge knowledge, specific solutions, your story.
   b. Process base: Method expert, facilitator, mediator, negotiator, teacher, and so on.
3. Are your assessment and action congruent?
   a. Are you trying to be a content expert when your real strength is process?
   b. Are you following the expertise that you want?
4. Are you making full use of your existing expertise?
   a. Are you utilizing it with audiences? Selecting the speeches that advance your expertise?
   b. Are you marketing yourself to your expertise?

Remember that in today's world of public speaking, you need to

- Develop an area of expertise.
- Know exactly what that expertise is.
- Constantly expand your expertise.
- Market yourself fully and honestly.
- Use the expertise to launch new paths.

CONNECT WITH YOUR UNIQUENESS

Step out and stand out from the growing crowd of look-alikes . . .

Tom Peters, *WOW*

Uniqueness means being one of a kind, unusual, or notable. Most people see themselves as less than unique, masking strengths and deflecting from skills with statements like "Oh, anyone could have done this job." Unique people are recognized as having a quality or talent that is only coined once.

On the bulletin board of my neighborhood copy center is a picture of a herd of black and white striped zebras with one standing out from the group in brilliant pink. It's impossible to look at the picture and not focus on the pink zebra. For speakers, maneuvering in an arena that drives us to stand out from the herd, our pursuit for uniqueness is often tied into trying to be a pink zebra, except that in a world of pink zebras, we risk loosing the uniqueness we seek. We can get into a crazy reverse "keeping up with the Joneses," continually scanning for what everyone else is doing so we can do something different.

Every speaker faces the challenge of impressing an audience, and the higher the competitive stakes, the more the demand for uniqueness. This distinction is built with two skills: (1) the skill of building a special connection with the audience; and (2) the skill of delivering your own unique gift.

Build the Special Connection

Some people have that ability to make others feel special; the natural talent of never meeting a stranger and being at home with every audience. It's an unquantifiable quality that projects "This is an important conversation; you are special." It has little to do with words or content; it's an intimate communication of the eye, voice, and presence; a distinctive and unmistakable essence that builds a personal bridge. Often years later someone reminds you of that special connection, "Remember *our* group? We were the ones who filled the room with balloons."

Give A Unique Gift

What can audiences rely on you to always give them? With what gifts are you consistently identified?

- High, valuable content?
- A new perspective?
- Cross-context examples that touch an audience personally and professionally?
- Great handouts?
- Practical, down-to-earth common sense?
- Serious teaching through humor?
- A great time?
- A good "kick in the _____" motivation?
- A memorable experience?
- Service that goes the extra mile?

Which are yours? What gifts distinguish you from other speakers? What is your signature?

Robert Thurman, professor of Indo-Tibetan Buddhist Studies at Columbia University and father of actress Uma Thurman, has a signature *presence*. His voice is like no other, a booming, reedy tenor that rises off at odd angles and zooms into open rhetorical space. He often sits cross-legged on the floor where few can see him and talks at such a rapid and uneven pace that he leaves you lost and scrambling to catch up. Yet, the real signature of this very popular and compelling speaker is his genius at teaching deep and serious concepts with humor. His principle gift is to disturb the surface of his audience and probe the deep with a laughing stick.

In my San Francisco neighborhood is a small Japanese restaurant called Moshi Moshi with an even smaller sushi/sake bar and five stools. One Tuesday afternoon, I watched Mits, the owner, with his five customers. His eyes danced as he poured sake from a small teapot and engaged them in discussions of ancient China, the reign of the Shoguns, and the philosophy of that time. A master with people, his face glowed as he shared his love of life with each person. Sake cups were never empty. An hour later, as they settled up their rather large sushi bills, each left with a happy face and the promise to return. I'm told that the stools are never empty when Mits tends bar.

If I asked Mits how he was unique, I think he would smile and shake his head. But having often observed him, I find the radiance of his smile and the sincerity he extends to people to be a rare gift. Mits gives people a unique experience, the experience of himself! There are many Japanese sushi bars in San Francisco, but only one where the customer feels so honored by the owner.

Carl Sandburg, the midwestern American poet, wrote a short poem in which he marveled at how millions of humans have lived on the planet, yet no two have the same thumb print. He humorously suggested that somewhere there must be a "great God of thumbs" who has it all catalogued. No matter how much alike we are, we each have a thumb print never to be duplicated.

Uniqueness is a paradox. The more we chase it, the more it eludes us. The more we attempt to find it outside of ourselves, in other people, the more we become like everyone else. The closer we come to our own thumb print, the more unique we are. The speaker who can comfortably and confidently present from the platform of that thumb print is powerful.

In a TV interview, the popular comedian Jerry Seinfeld revealed, "I'm not trying to make it, I'm trying to do something right." Seinfeld played himself, presenting a real person, authentic and available to his audience. In doing this, he outdistanced all his competition.

Examine your own signature, your own thumb! Once you know it and learn to honor it, your uniqueness will unfold and lead you to presentation and speaking results beyond your expectation.

SO, WHAT DO YOU BRING TO THE PARTY?

It was written of Barbra Streisand in a review of her one-woman concert that for all her pseudo-openness, she stayed hidden behind a dazzling curtain of artifice and technique. A great artist and a unique talent, she was perceived by one reviewer as not bringing herself "fully" to the party. As you get in touch with your stories, your expertise, and your uniqueness, you build that sense of self that allows you to bring yourself unrestrictively to the audience. As you release your mask, remove blinders, and expand your platform, the magic of your treasures becomes more fully available to you and to others.

This is your *platform:* your treasure chest of stories, expert skills, knowledge, and uniqueness. To be a speaker of impact, you must privately step down off the platform and meet up with your message and your passion. You'll find them somewhere in that fourth part of your window, your *source* (see Figure 3.2).

Figure 3.2

The Speaker's Platform and Source

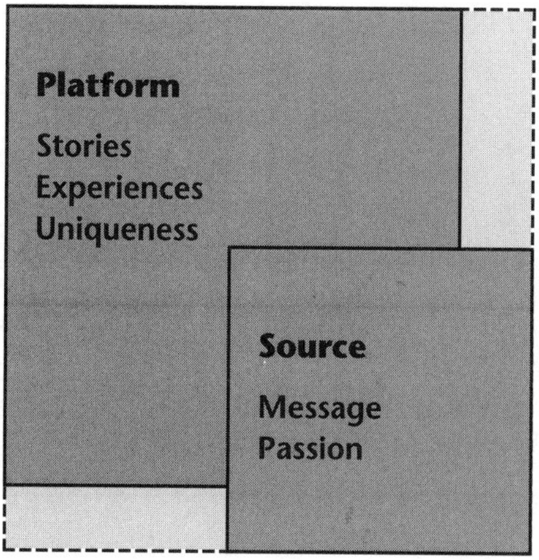

Platform

Stories
Experiences
Uniqueness

Source

Message
Passion

4 WHAT IS YOUR MESSAGE?

Find a Simple Dwelling in the Center of a Complex World

The house lights dim.
Center stage
A single actor
Turns on a tape recorder.
That's it!
That's the entire drama!
What a lot of *krap!*

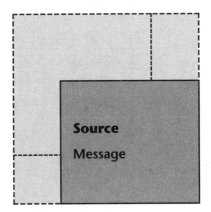

Edward Albee's *Krapp's Last Tape* was written for the Theater of the Absurd movement of the 1950s: one character, Krapp, one small table, a tape recorder, and an audience subjected to an hour of prerecorded voice. Is there a message here?

Author Dave Peizer, in a recent newspaper interview, put in his own graphic terms, "That's why I don't like these motivational speakers. They throw on a switch or read somebody else's words."

Like Krapp, some speakers sound like a prerecorded message. Others turn everything into a message, straining to find a deeper meaning that can lead one to say

I should be content
To look at a mountain for what it is
And not as a comment on life.

Some speakers leave us with the impression that *they* are the message! And some speakers who prefer to give this message assignment to the motivational types, see themselves more as the messenger who brings information, expertise, and solutions. All of this opens the old question about messages and messengers: What's the distinction?

DON'T SHOOT THE MESSENGER!

A messenger is someone who prepares the way. In medieval times, the messenger was sent ahead of the advancing army to find safe lodging for the troops. In classical Greek plays, the messenger was often the character who came on stage to let the audience know that an action had already occurred offstage. Of course, this all sounds quite modern; speakers and trainers being hired to pave the way for decisions already implemented or to motivate and bring employees into line who might sabotage the already advancing army of change.

Messenger is also the name for a line used in hauling, as between two ships. It's a rope or chain that is passed around a capstan (a machine for moving heavy objects) with the ends lashed together to form a loop. A great metaphor for the speaker, facilitator, presenter: You build a loop around your-self and the audience so that you can move a heavy object—a shift in perspective, a breakthrough in knowledge, a change in response. You are the messenger, and your message is the line that forms the loop!

EVERY SPEAKER HAS A MESSAGE

Wait a minute, now you've gone too far!

- "I don't have a message; I deal with facts and problem identification."
- "What I present are briefings and reports that speak for themselves. Any message is in the content"
- "I'm strictly a process person. I help people connect with their own needs. I don't come with my message; I listen for theirs."

Whether you realize it or not, you have a message. It's the core of all your communication, the logo that underlies your content, what you're really passionate about. Underneath the facts, the logic, the supporting materials is a "simple dwelling"—a single, powerful imperative that has so much meaning to you that it drives every communication. It's where you are coming from and where you're going. You are the messenger connected to your message, and to know this message is to open the door to impact with an audience.

How to Find Your Message

One simple question can lead you to your message: *What's important?* Each time you ask this question, you move yourself to another layer of meaning, and each layer takes you one step closer to your message. I'll demonstrate the technique.

Karen O'Brien designs Web sites and markets this service to clients. As we sat over coffee, I took her through the process of finding her message by first asking her for the title of one of her presentations; she suggested "Electronic Commerce," an hour-long speech about doing business by e-mail.

> **Nice:** What's important about speaking on this subject?
> **O'Brien:** That the audience leave with an understanding of how it works.
> **Nice:** What's important about the audience leaving with this understanding?
> **O'Brien:** I want them to be pro e-mail.
> **Nice:** What's important about them being pro e-mail?
> **O'Brien:** They can spread that awareness to others.
> **Nice:** What's important about spreading that awareness to others?
> **O'Brien:** They can share their experiences.
> **Nice:** What's important about sharing *your* experiences?
> **O'Brien:** Someone appreciates your knowledge. You *contribute!*

She said "contribute" like someone, after a long journey, finally reaching home. I knew we had reached her message. I asked her for a second topic, preferably very different, and she chose a talk given for a personal development program on "Life Experiences."

> **Nice:** What was the message in that talk?
> **O'Brien:** That life can change in a second.
> **Nice:** What's important about knowing life can change in a second?
> **O'Brien:** Not to get too comfortable.
> **Nice:** What's important about not getting too comfortable?
> **O'Brien:** You live life more consciously, more aware.

Nice: What's important about living more consciously, more aware?

O'Brien: You appreciate what you have. You don't get lost in the day-to-day.

Nice: What's important about not getting lost in the day-to-day?

O'Brien: You get to feel!

Nice: What's important about getting to feel?

O'Brien: Without feeling, there's no purpose in life.

Nice: And for what purpose is feeling?

O'Brien: It allows me to know who I am.

Nice: And what does knowing who you are allow you to do?

O'Brien: To take care of myself.

Nice: And when you know who you are and can take care of yourself, what's important then? What does that free you to do?

O'Brien: I'm free to *contribute.*

These were two very different topics, yet the same match lit each pyre. Her inner message was the same for both. Take careful note of the progression it took to uncover this match.

Topic: "Electronic Commerce"	Topic: "Life Experiences"
Stated message: *E-mail is a viable way of doing business.*	Stated message: *Life can change in a second.*
What's important?	**What's important?**
To understand how it works	To not get too comfortable
To be pro e-mail	To live consciously, more aware
To spread awareness to others	To not get lost in the day-to-day
To share experiences	To feel
To contribute	To know purpose in life
	To know who I am
	To take care of myself
	To contribute

No matter what topic she chooses, Karen O'Brien will take it to "contribution." The more she is in conscious touch with this inner message, the stronger her impact will be.

Your Multiple Message

Each speaker has three messages: a content message, a result message, and an inner message. The content message is what you say; the result message is where you want the content to take your audience and the level of impact you are going for. The inner message is what fuels both. In the preparation stage, you should clearly identify and integrate each message; any incongruency will hinder impact. Note Karen's O'Brien's three messages:

	Electronic Commerce	**Life Experiences**
Content Message	E-mail is a viable way of doing business.	Life can change in a second.
Result Message	Bring audiences to an understanding of how it works.	Bring audiences to conscious awareness.
Internal Message	It's important to *contribute* knowledge to others.	Awareness frees me to *contribute*.

Suppose O'Brien is giving a marketing presentation. If she feels that she cannot make a major contribution to this organization, no matter what she targeted for content and result, the impact of her presentation would be flat. If midway into the job she finds her contribution thwarted or unappreciated, she will do less than her best work. In the larger professional picture, she will do her best with audiences and clients who understand contribution and appreciate hers. She will speak on topics that showcase contribution and will have the most impact with clients who give her the freedom to make a significant contribution to them.

Annette Martin is a friend and colleague with 16 years of experience with Naval Media Services at Pearl Harbor, Hawaii. On a recent drive together from San Francisco to Santa Cruz, I practiced this technique with her, asking her for three topics, as different as she could make them.

Her first topic was "Getting Clear." I first asked her what she thought were her *content* and *result messages*. Here immediate answers were, "I'd talk about the importance of simplifying one's life and getting priorities clear. I'd want people to identify and act on at least one priority in their own life."

Nice: What's important about simplifying life and getting priorities clear?

Martin: Being open to possibilities.

Nice: What's important about being open to possibilities?

Martin: Receiving what comes to you.

Nice: And what's important about receiving what comes to you?

Martin: That's when you listen to your heart.

Nice: And what's important about listening to your heart?

Martin: Because we're all learning and receiving from each other.

Nice: What's important about learning and receiving from each other?

Martin: *We're all responsible for each other.*

Her second topic was "The Hawaiian Monk Seal." Knowing that she had produced a film on Midway Island about returning the island back to the wildlife, I suggested she consider her next audience to be the Nature Conservatory in Honolulu.

Nice: What would be your *content message?*

Martin: I'd talk about how the monk seal's habitat has

been diminished and how to get the seal back to the original islands. I want people to know how they can be involved.

Nice: What would be your primary *result message?*

Martin: I want everyone to get involved.

Nice: What's important about speaking on the monk seal?

Martin: That we take action to ensure their survival.

Nice: What's important about their survival?

Martin: They are a part of our whole—the living system on this planet.

Nice: What's important about concern for the "whole?"

Martin: We're all one: *We're all responsible for each other.*

Nice: Great! Notice what happened. Both topics took you to this same core message. Speaking from this message would give you a lot of energy!

Martin: Yes, because they would be getting *me.*

Her third topic was "How to Produce a Film." Her audience would be film students. Her *content message* to them would be that they first have to decide what they want to communicate through their film. Her *result message* would be for them to examine the film they are presently making and decide what they want to say.

Nice: What's important about making this decision at the beginning?

Martin: Otherwise, they'll waste time on unrelated materials; everything has to support the whole.

Nice: So your message is what?

Martin: That they have a responsibility to the public.

Nice: Because . . . ?

Martin: Yes, because *we are responsible—to and for each other.*

Nice: Is there any doubt about what your message is?

Regardless of content or subject matter, it's *your* essential truth.

Martin: This is great! This is my work! This isn't new to me, but I never realized it quite so strongly! *It all comes together.* Now I know what I want to communicate!

Nice: You got all of this through what we did just now?

Martin: Yeah!!

Note her three messages:

	Getting Clear	**Hawaiian Monk Seal**	**How to Produce a Film**
Content Message	It's important to simplify your life and get your priorities clear.	Habitat has been diminished; how to re-store the seal to the original islands.	In producing a film, you must first decide what you want to communicate.
Result Message	Identify and act on at least one priority in your life.	Everyone in the audience is to get involved.	Examine the film you are presently making and decide what you want to say.
Internal Message	We're all re-sponsible for each other.	We're all re-sponsible for each other.	We're all re-sponsible for each other.

Note the process that I used with both Karen O'Brien and Annette Martin. This is a technique you can use with yourself or better yet, in dialogue with another, when you are (1) selecting a topic; (2) preparing your talk; (3) not sure where you're going with a talk; and (4) double-checking your own effectiveness.

To find your message:

1. Identify the topic and the audience.
2. Start with your content message; what do you want to get across?
3. What's important about either the topic or the content message?
4. Keep with the "what's important" questions until you start hearing repeat answers or you hit a layer that has real juice for you. Ride the horse as far as it goes.

Don't stress or think too hard about your answers. This is not about being right; it's about saying what comes into your mind. Use a tape recorder and transcribe your answers; note the words and phrases that you use. If you don't reach a message, put it away, and try again when you're fresh. The important thing is not to try. This is a trip into your unknown; go gently, and take more than one path. Allow your intuitive side to lead.

> Your message does not come from your head.
> It is not knowledge based.
> Call it your heart, your gut, your soul,
> It's your essential truth.
> It doesn't have to be a grand passion,
> It can be a core belief.
> It is unique to you.
> It's where you are coming from!

> Your message unfolds.
> You do not build it, it's already there.
> You just have to uncover it, clear the debris . . .
> Examine what you think you know
> Remove the layers
> Dig around.
> When you hit it
> You will know it!
> Like striking pay dirt!
> Like coming home!
> Everything in you will say "Yes"
> This is it!

5 WHERE IS YOUR PASSION?

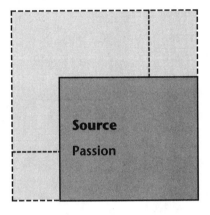

> *Dwell as near as possible to the channel in which your life flows.*
>
> Henry David Thoreau

A man once asked Louis Armstrong, "Brother, what is jazz?" Louis replied, "Brother, if you got to ask, You ain't got it!"

Passion can send one man on a bicycle around the world, another into an archeological dig, and a third to developing Web sites; it can even take a woman into speaking to audiences. It's your passion that wakes up the slumbering zeal of an audience. When passion meets passion, impact happens! People work harder, take risks, make changes. What exactly is passion? Well, brother, if you've got it, you know it, and if you ain't, you're just another talking dud.

DISCONNECTING IN WHITE WATER

In his book *Management as a Performing Art*, Peter Vaill compares living in the working world to navigating permanent white water: plummeting from crisis to crisis, trying to avoid rocks and overturning, while all the time snagged to a bottom line of schedule, deadlines, mortgage, and jobs. In a crisis environment, passion is reined in to the service of staying topside, and, locked into this burden, people get scared, lose their vision, and sometimes pull the plug. We've seen the spirit go out of whole institutions, young people living without dreams, and seniors docilely taking the golden handshake of encouraged early retirement. Eventually, disconnection feels normal, and people forget what it was to be alive!

It's hard to stay in touch with inspiration when battling white water. As speakers, we can lose our vision as our focus goes to finding the next audience. Uncertainty can lock us into taking every speaking possibility. Audiences can drain us, and, as we try to light the fires of others, our own flame dampens in the details of living. It's so subtle—this disconnection from the joy, the excitement, and the wonder that brought us here. We function, and we look successful, but isolation sets in as we work out of a home office and lose touch with the coworkers we used to see every day. The spontaneity goes out of our lives, and a gradual numbness creeps in as we feel less and push harder. And then we find ourselves writing in a journal that ten years ago, we looked away for a moment and it became our life.

Audiences share the same potential for disconnection. They can lose touch with early vitality as they release their dreams and settle for just doing their jobs. Isolation and overwhelm can cause them to fence off their feelings and settle for more confined and predictable paths. The job of the speaker is to break through the numbness, fuse the isolated ends together, and fix the disconnection. The speaker is the conduit who sets up the power supply system for the audience. When energies flow, impact happens! Speakers recharge, audiences connect with themselves, and everyone lights into a single energy as together they navigate the rapids, enjoying the same insights and laughs. This connection begins with you, with your own clarity and the work you do to open your own energy channels. Content is anchored at a far deeper level than face-value information. If this deeper level is missing in the speaker, the audience has no choice but to stay at the surface. There is no faking this! Only to the degree that you are in touch with your own passions, only to that benchmark, can your audience come.

CONNECTING WITH YOUR PASSION

Find Your Pulse

Mary Catherine Bateson, daughter of anthropologists Margaret Mead and Gregory Bateson, in her book *Composing a Life* says that we connect with our passion "when we touch the private spaces of our lives where the spirit flourishes and the woods are still wild." So often, this connection comes when we feel most free: moments of simplicity like walking a beach, polishing a vintage car, sleeping out under the stars, watching a sunset, smelling fresh-cut grass, playing with our children. We hear ourselves in the silent places: skiing a mountain, walking through a redwood forest or becoming one with the soundless glide of the sail. We know passionate stillness in prayer and meditation, in yoga and reflection. We meet someone who lights a connection; we find ourselves at the center of an event that opens doors, a creative project takes us to our essence. Sometimes it takes a dangerous diagnosis or catastrophe to wake us out of our numbness and feel the beat of our own pulse. In the wild woods we discover what is really important in our lives and with that knowing we face an audience, charged by our passion and grounded in that our power. That's when we speak for impact.

Pulse Finders

Donna Hartley was returning from winning the Miss Hawaii title when her plane burst into flames on the Los Angeles runway and, within seconds, she was faced with the most critical decision of her life: to die or to live! Consciously choosing to live, she plunged through the flames to an exit. She was one of the few survivors and is now using this dramatic event to introduce her powerful message on being fully alive.

Jason Lewis of Dorchester, England, graduated from university and floated in and out of a series of jobs looking for something that would capture his wit and energy. He met up with a friend who was pedaling a small boat across the Atlantic and decided to join him. Somewhere in the middle of the Atlantic Ocean, around day 80 of this tedious journey, Jason recalls: "There was a four-minute period when it seemed like everything just ripped away and I had total understanding. It was the most lucid experience of my life, everything made sense. I felt a part of everything, total acceptance. It came from within me and locked into everything around me, the boat, the ocean, the entire universe." After 111 days, with no clothes and no remaining food, they made it to Miami; Jason walked back into society grounded and more alive. Now, he speaks to young people on "living their dream."

Beth Urech reconnected with a lifelong passion when she finished initial parenting. A public speaking professor in Chicago, she had married a Swiss lawyer, moved to Zurich, and raised two children. When her family duties lessened, she started looking for another career. Since her passion had always been the speaking platform, she started speaking and has built a thriving business coaching executives who speak internationally.

Padi Selwyn met someone who opened her door to a new vision. She had run a full-service advertising and public relations company for 14 years and was always speaking at local events to promote her business. She told me that one day after a Rotary presentation, a man in the audience said to her, "I've just come back from a big national convention, and you're a better speaker than all the ones I heard there. You should do this professionally!" She did and is now a highly successful speaker, author, and past president of the Northern California National Speakers Association.

Speaking for impact means never taking your fingers off the pulse—yours, the audience's, and that of the world around you. You may feel the pulse beat through a cause, a new perspective, a personal sharing, or a teaching. It may be a vision of how things might be or information so important that it must be shared. If you reach a day when you don't feel the pulse, stop right there and find it. You can't lose it, it's always with you—you've just forgotten where to touch. Life is too short to live without that touch.

Renew Your Vows

A few years ago, I was invited to the wedding anniversary of two friends who had been married to each other for 45 years. It was complete with church, wedding dress, pink champagne, and a California earthquake that shook the church! It was a time for restirring the passion.

There is an energy in vows:

- I'm going to be a speaker.
- I promise myself never to give less than my best.
- I will be available to people.
- I will never stop learning.

It's professionally healthy to return to early vows every so often and reconfirm to yourself why you choose to do this. If you lose touch with your earlier enthusiasm, if you're contemplating a shift in focus, and, especially, if you're a beginning speaker, take time to reexamine your "why." It will take you back to your reasons for speaking and alert you to anything that might be missing. It will reconfirm the rightness of your choices and reconnect you with that early spark.

GET IN TOUCH WITH YOUR *WHY!*

I find three reasons why speakers speak. Every successful speaker indulges in all three but there is usually one essential reason why you're in this game.

1. You feel *alive.*
2. You get *action.*
3. You get *dividends.*

1. Feeling Alive!

I speak because I'm happy! I speak because I'm free!
My eye is on the audience, and I know they're loving me!

Life can be on the rocks, but in front of an audience you dance! Your life may be one disruption after another, but with an audience you feel in control, organized, and focused. Even if your heart pounds before a talk, once you start the tension releases, the adrenaline pumps in, and you're airborne. You love the high; it's definitely addictive. Where some people would rather face a firing squad than an audience, it's just the reverse for you; just give you an audience, and you're flying.

Do you speak because you're alive, or do you
speak to come alive?

What Brings You to Life?

To what do you attribute that aliveness when you speak?
Check out the following, and see what fits for you.

_____ 1. *The audience itself,* the shared energy.

_____ 2. *Organization and preparation.* You feel uncertain and
tend to shut down aliveness when not well prepared.
Winging it is terrifying; your freedom comes when
you know, going in, that you are well prepared.

_____ 3. *Being impromptu.* You feel most alive when you can
throw away the script.

_____ 4. *Dialogue.* You do your best when you can interact
with the audience. You're brilliant when you can
bounce off the responses of others.

_____ 5. *Humor.* This frees you up and gets you comfortable.
You really bloom if you can break the seriousness
and get the audience smiling.

_____ 6. *Repetition.* When you know a talk so well that it's a
part of you, you have real freedom on the stage.
Mastery brings energy.

_____ 7. *A prop.* You do best when backed by slides, video,
handouts, trinkets for the audience; it just feels kind
of alone up there without some tactile supports.

_____ 8. *Passion for the subject.* You need to really be into it.

_____ 9. *Creativity.* It's the artist in you.

Prioritize

Considering everything that contributes to your sense of aliveness with audiences, write down what is the most essential, the most important? Then, list in priority the other ingredients that free up your aliveness.

Most Important
   For full aliveness during my talk: _____

Important (list three):

_____

_____

_____

What Do Your Choices Say to You?

■ If organization and preparation affect your aliveness with an audience, make sure you have time and access to resources for the quality work you want. Don't try to beat it; don't give the presentation unless you're comfortable with your preparation.

■ If being impromptu is where you shine, then work from an outline instead of a fully scripted talk. Take every opportunity to make full advantage of speaker/audience *dialogue*. Look for ways, no matter how static the situation, to get response and to break the monologue format. Be creative!

■ If humor keeps you comfortable, you're no doubt a natural, and when you're fully alive humor probably flows. This can be your signature, even if you are a serious content speaker. Just because it comes naturally doesn't mean you shouldn't perfect it. Develop a resource of materials, practice uncovering humor in all situations, and work on your timing!

■ If you thrive on repetition, you might want to look to generic public programs where your presentation can be more set. This moves you closer to performance and away

from customizing and adapting. Many seminar companies offer these opportunities.

Are You an Audience Junkie?

There's a little junkie in all of us; we love the alive feeling
when speaking! There are, however, speakers who only feel
alive when performing, who really need that audience. There's
nothing wrong with enjoying the trip, but, if you're hooked
on the thrill of the ride, it's an unsound basis for impact. To
anyone seriously addicted to audiences, consider moving
beyond this dependency. Insist on more balance in your life,
discover your message, and take your audience connection to a
new level beyond the fix to a mutual benefit. You won't lose
the high; it actually gets better. You don't need to go through
an audience to feel aliveness; you can go directly!

2. Taking Action!

You get to drive the car!

You never were much for bouncing along in the back seat.
You want the steering wheel where you can see what's going
on, where you can make a contribution, be a voice for
change, improve conditions, make the world a better place,
and be a part of the solution. Logically, action keeps your life
on track; emotionally, it fuels your energy.

Do you speak because you get to be
the driver and choose the route?

What Actions Turn You On?

I love to drive narrow, winding, steep roads, especially 90
degree curves. What are the roads that bring you to life? Read
through the following eight challenges, and check the actions
that showcase your own aliveness.

_____ 1. *Making your talk personal.* You are most effective when you can bring yourself into the speech: a personal feeling, story, example.

_____ 2. *Taking it to the big picture.* It's important to always show how parts connect to the whole.

_____ 3. *Finding a new perspective.* You're always looking for a new way, a different treatment, a fresh outlook.

_____ 4. *Finding a solution.* Answers and solutions are where you always head.

_____ 5. *Identifying change.* You always look for what can be changed.

_____ 6. *Beginnings and endings:* You thrive on the freshness of the startup and the satisfaction of the finish, so you can go on to another beginning.

_____ 7. *Give and take.* You are at your best when actively involved with audience participation.

_____ 8. *Challenging your audience.* You like to stretch their knowledge and experience, keep them on their toes, kick them up into a new sphere. You dare them to take the challenge.

Prioritize!

Now, considering all the actions that contribute to your feeling of aliveness with audiences, which one is the most essential, the mother lode for you? Write it down and then prioritize other actions that give you energy.

Most Important Action:

_____

Important Actions (list three):

_____

_____

_____

What Do These Choices Say to You?

The actions you choose point to what you need to be doing in your speeches. If the excitement has gone out of your speaking, you may not be recognizing what keeps you vital.

■ If making it personal brings your speaking to life, then speak to audiences who want this sharing. If you leave this element out because you think the audience won't accept it, this adaptation could cancel out impact because what fuels *your* energy is missing. Look for appropriate ways to include your passion that will be accepted and welcomed by each audience.

■ If finding new perspectives and taking it to the big picture are your energy sources, then you'll have more fun talking to innovators, planners, marketing and sales people—audiences that speak the big picture language. It's hard to take in-the-moment action people to a master plan.

■ If answers and solutions ignite your passion, you'll do well with most audiences. In Part III, Chapters 6 and 7, you'll learn how to adapt answers and solutions to every audience.

■ If change is essential, then choose engagements where change is possible. Some audiences are notorious for smiling faces and no action. Some clients use speakers as window dressing to help them appear innovative with no intention of action. Companies are known for bringing in speakers to motivate their lower-level employees with no intention of giving support from the top. Tell your audiences what they must do to make a change. Speak to areas where some change is possible, or define your results so that you can recognize some element of change. Set it up so you get feedback.

■ If audience give-and-take is where you shine, then work it into every presentation, even lectures.

3. Cashing Dividends!

Laughing all the way to the bank!

You don't have to go to the bank to cash in the dividends of applause, appreciation, recognition, travel, meeting new people, love, acceptance, and never having to be bored. Of all the possible dividends, three are especially important to speakers:

1. Meaning
2. Challenge
3. Personal growth

Meaning: First Dividend

What you say has relevance. To rephrase Maslow, when your tool is a hammer, you get to hit the nail on the head, and when the audience confirms it, you hit the jackpot. Someone thanks you or tells you they still remember how you helped them through a crisis. I remember a manager who told me that the direction of his career was set by a talk I gave years earlier, and I remember hearing that a team-building group was still getting together some ten years later. These are the jewels that sparkle in your memory. Yo Yo Ma, the world-famous cellist, said it with simplicity and passion in his documentary, *Finding Your Voice,* "There is nothing so exciting as when I see that someone gets it!" It's instant gratification when faces light up and audiences break into spontaneous applause. You do your best work with audiences who mirror back an appreciative positive response. You slowly die when your meaning doesn't make it.

Is this a dividend you have to have?

Challenge: Second Dividend

Barbara Walters, in a TV interview with the actor Woody Harrelson, asked him why he became an actor. His answer, "Because it scared the ____ out of me." Do you find yourself taking the tough routes and tackling audiences that others say are impossible? Do you do your best work when terrified? I remember the challenge of speaking through an interpreter for the first time, trying to get a win/win message across to warring educators on Guam, and facing a group of expressionless delinquents at a correctional home for teenage boys. If you're hooked on challenge you're hooked for life because there's always another one waiting in the wings.

Does your passion for speaking come from the challenge?

Personal Growth: Third Dividend

What do *you* get to take home? Do you pick topics because of what you will learn yourself? Is it personal growth and change that draws you? Do you leave a topic when you have learned it? Speakers who demand learning from every talk find it hard to repeat themselves. Even when a speech is practiced and precisely crafted, something has to be new for the speaker. Yo Yo Ma told his students, "You must be different every time: You cannot create, practice, and make 100 copies." For speakers who demand learning and growth, there is no automatic pilot; it's always a first time.

Is personal growth an imperative for you?

What Dividends Do You Want?

Combine the three dividends: meaning, challenge, personal growth.

_____ 1. *Mastering new information.* You want to continually expand your knowledge and world vision.

_____2. *Money and fame.* You want to make big money and be well known in your professional field.

_____3. *Acknowledgment and appreciation.* You really need to hear words of appreciation, acknowledgment from your peers, and positive feedback from an audience.

_____4. *Seeing your own speaking growth.* You need the realization of how far you've come. You need to see and feel personal improvement.

_____5. *Seeing change.* It's important that your speech hit some mark, that something changes with the audience. It doesn't need to be a big change, but you need to see some shift.

_____6. *Making a difference.* You need to know that you're making a difference in someone's life, contributing to the greater good.

_____7. *Inner growth.* One of the major reasons you speak is to aid your own personal growth. Speaking teaches you about who you are and how to relate with people.

_____8. *Challenge, adventure, risk.* Once you've mastered a topic, you have to move on. You need the rush that comes from challenge and the sense of mastery when you make it.

_____9. *Acceptance and belonging.* You need to feel accepted by the audience. Inclusion is important.

Prioritize

You may cash in on all three major dividends: meaning, challenge, and personal growth. But ask yourself, what is the most important one. Without it, I would not be speaking or be in this job? Write it down and then prioritize three additional dividends that you count on.

Most Important

_____

Important (list three):

_____

_____

_____

WHAT DO THESE CHOICES SAY TO YOU?

Meaning

> *Acknowledgment, appreciation, making a difference, acceptance, and belonging*

Audience feedback is essential to you, as immediate as possible. You need personal communication with your audience; you need to hear, see, and experience the results of your connection. Too many concurrent sessions with people moving in and out at the back of the room can leave you drained. Evaluations that go first to the client may have cooled by the time they reach you. The structure of a meeting may not allow time or opportunity to actually talk with your audience. Rushing from one talk to another, grabbing airport limos, and running for flights with no time for immediate feedback can be emotionally depleting. When caught in these situations, consciously set up feedback structures for the audience to reach you. It's your nourishment; don't be without it.

If you want to be appreciated and enjoy a sense of belonging in your speaking, pick your groups carefully. International audiences may be responsive in different ways and not as openly talkative as you're used to in the United States. Bottom-line bosses who get low marks in positive reinforcement may not express their appreciation even though they feel your impact. Powerless people with low self-esteem can be brutal on evaluation sheets. If you do your best work with the warm fuzzies, then build your niche with these empathetic people. Explore your skills with other audiences, but just remember where your soup kitchen is.

Challenge

> *Money, fame, challenge, change, adventure, and risk*

If you think fame and fortune are there for you, go for it! Establishing a name for yourself, packaging and promoting an idea or expertise, and making the decision to go for the bigger bucks can bring a tremendous high. However, if you think that money is your turn-on, it's more likely tied to challenge than to dollars. There's not a lot of juice in money alone without the other rewards.

If adventure and risk are your snap-crackle-and-pop breakfast cereal, then don't get stuck with Shredded Wheat. Go for the chance to talk to that audience of 4,000 people, figure out how to fulfill the client's crazy dream of an underwater presentation, come up with something no one else has done, do it and talk about it. Dare to be wild, take an unpopular stance on a current issue: Just keep your world charged and challenged.

Personal Growth

> *Mastery, professional and personal improvement, inner strength, and knowledge*

Speaking to audiences is a personal journey. No matter how obscure and impersonal your topic, it's your person that gets up there and delivers. Whether you take this dividend or not, it accrues for you with every talk with compounded interest, figured daily!

Look at Your Full Picture

In each of the areas, aliveness, action, and dividends, what did you write as your most important ingredient? Then, what were your priority choices? Bring everything together and look at it.

Aliveness	Action	Dividends
Most Important	*Most Important*	*Most Important*
_____	_____	_____
_____	_____	_____
Important	*Important*	*Important*
1. _____	1. _____	1. _____
_____	_____	_____
2. _____	2. _____	2. _____
_____	_____	_____
3. _____	3. _____	3. _____
_____	_____	_____

As you take this fuller look at yourself, realize what each category tells you about your reasons for speaking.

■ *Aliveness:* These are what turn you on, what excite you, where the juice lies.

■ *Action:* These are probably what you do best, your strengths.

■ *Dividends:* These are the rewards that are most meaningful to you.

I've been taking a look at myself while writing this chapter. To give you a fuller perspective on the picture of your own choices, here is my picture and my own interpretations of it.

Aliveness	Action	Dividends
Most Important	*Most Important*	*Most Important*
To be creative	To bring a new perspective	To make a significant contribution
Important	*Important*	*Important*
1. Well prepared	1. Big picture	1. Acknowledgment
2. Impromptu	2. Personalize	2. Make a difference
3. Audience dialogue	3. Give-and-take	3. Find meaning

Most important to me as a speaker:

■ The chance to be creative is what turns me on and brings me to life.
■ When I can work in a new perspective, I am at my best.
■ Making a contribution is the dividend that I most treasure.

Important in keeping my passion alive. My content should:

■ Offer a new perspective.
■ Be meaningful to me and others.
■ Make some small contribution to the audience, the world.
■ Be thoroughly prepared.

My process works best when:

■ Personalized.
■ Impromptu.
■ Involving dialogue, give and take, with the audience.

This is why I speak; these are the doors to my passion. Look again, now, at your own choices. You have written your own prescription for emotional maintenance and personal power. Listen to your inner voice. When selecting a speech topic, developing a presentation, accepting a speaking engagement, or customizing for a client, keep your choices as close as you can to your passion.

Get passionate about the results you can accomplish. If you want to swim in the Olympics and you stay too long in the beginner's pool you'll lose your passion and if you commit yourself to the impossible you'll burn out trying. Find your own balance between challenge and success. If your account gets overdrawn, look for what you are not depositing. Take responsibility for nurturing the passion that takes you to impact with others.

SPEAKING FROM THE HEART

The secret of being a bore is to tell everything.

Voltaire

As I surfed channels with the TV remote, I accidentally hit on a straggly looking young woman angrily confronting a sprawled- and spaced-out young man on one of our morning talk shows, amplifying the worst of the current fad to tell it all. This trend to reveal all often gets confused in some speaking styles that speak from the heart.

Indulgence or Cop Out?

Just being practical, there are good reasons why heart talk is popular.

1. *It's easy!* It's easier to be an expert on your own heart, easier to remember your lines and be spontaneous; if you forget, you can improvise.
2. *It's safe!* It's safer to stay in your own pool and forget the ocean, especially if you're not a great swimmer.
3. *It feeds the ego!* Some have the mistaken assumption that the only way to reach hearts is through your own heart. "I'm connected with me, isn't everyone? I get to be expert and authority."

I was talking with David Garfinkel on this subject and found his observations to be right to the point: "I think there's an assumption that my heart is smarter than anything, so when I find something I love, doesn't everyone want to hear about it? It's sort of like 'his majesty the baby.' Now it may be there's a whole bunch of budgets in the 21st century reserved for from-the-heart speakers, but I think a lot of people are misusing the notion to sell books and to self-indulge.

Do Audiences Want Your Heart?

No!

Audiences do not want you to surgically open your heart and serve it every time you speak. They're tired of bleeding hearts following their bliss on the audience's time. They're impatient with dumpers who use them to work through their own therapy. They want substance: content appropriate to their needs and interests. They want structure: a talk that takes them somewhere. They want heart. Their own!

Yes!

Audiences need to know you have a heart! They want dynamic energy, personal conviction, and a heartfelt laugh. Even bottom-line audiences want to get to the "heart of the matter." Impact with an audience means coming from that heart and creating a "heart-to-heart," even when the setting is formal, factual, and fine tuned. As with the Tin Man in *The Wizard of Oz,* the yellow brick road must take you to your heart.

You Got to Have Heart!

Two people come to mind as I write. One is a woman who has an educational TV series on art history, a Roman Catholic nun who goes by the name of Sister Wendy. Her voice is thin, her subject trails into obscure details about unrenowned paintings, and the camera freezes on her alone, just talking. But there is something about her that negates dismissal. In fact, I find myself drawn in, listening intently to a subject that never interested me before. Her untrained voice and dancing eyes are infectious; her enthusiasm is so contagious that I'm *really* looking at these paintings. It's not the content or even the enthusiasm that holds me; it's her love for this work that comes through. She transforms remote content into an intensely personal revelation of her own intimate discoveries. I can read this stuff in art history books, but she takes me by the hand and leads me through her own unique treasures. And she does this without ever talking about herself! The gift she brings us is her passion.

The second person takes me back to my graduate days at Northwestern University and to a retired civil engineer in his 70s whom we all called Mr. Charlie. Mr. Charlie had a passion for classical music and constructed elaborate presentations on the classical masters. On Friday nights, in the small Chicago apartment that he shared with his bachelor son, Mr. Charlie would present his programs, always to a packed house! This was before CDs and sophisticated audio-visual equipment; he had a record player, walls of multicolored hand-printed flip-chart sheets—and his own love of music. He mumbled and often got lost in his notes, he defied all the rules for even adequate presenting, yet hundreds of people chose to spend their Friday nights, crammed into this bare-bones bachelor apartment, sitting on uncomfortable folding chairs, listening to an old man speak from his heart. I actually learned a lot on those Friday nights and now, years later, I remember Mr. Charlie doing what he loved. He never gave a personal story, never shared his life, he just glowed! His impact on me was permanent, and his gift is still unfolding.

> **Padi Selwyn:** I think you have to love your audience to be good. I think one big mistake speakers make is to tell gut-wrenching stories when there is no point. Tell me what the learning is, don't just jerk my emotions around. I really have a problem with speakers who use their illnesses, their tragedies to make an audience cry or open their hearts and then not take them anywhere or find a benefit from it for the audience. It just manipulates the audience; there's no point to it. I consider myself the hired help. I do! I schlep my books around, and I get jet lag. No matter what kind of fees a speaker gets, remember you're the hired help, you're there to do a job. Everything you do has to relate to the point!

Speak to Their Heart

"Heart talk" is speaking from your passion and message—to the passion and message of your audience. For the speaker to use personal examples and stories is entirely appropriate if they fit the passion and message of the audience. I'm talking about a congruent presentation that integrates your inner message with substance and a structure that connects the audience to their own self-image, their view of the world, their mastery, their pride and their pain, their purpose, what's really important to them. There's the heart of the matter! It's the subtle shift of connecting your own heart beat with the beat of the audience. David Garfinkel said it all in one simple statement: "Maybe the leap we need to make is to be passionate about what the other person really needs!"

> Find the collective heart!
> Go beyond yourself
> To their passion and message.
> Build that heart connection!
> And you have
> Impact!

CARRIERS OF SPIRIT

> Playing music is supposed to be fun.
> It's not about notes on a page.
> It's about being alive!
>
> Richard Dreyfus, in the film *Mr. Holland's Opus*

One thing about jazz, it's alive! It starts where it starts and goes where it goes. Jazz is not about notes on a page, it's about the spirit that connects. It's not about being perfect or accomplishing something great; it's about a simple structure and the freedom to go anywhere!

Jazz isn't about where you start from,
it's about where you can go!

For the speaker, all doors are open. Even well-rehearsed performances need those impromptu moments when a familiar theme comes from the audience and you go with it. Your impact will never be measured by how perfectly you play the score but by how you strengthen and reinforce the human element within yourself and your audience. You are carriers of spirit whether you teach marketing, help people define goals, or analyze zero-based budgeting. Speakers cover a wide range of potentially lifeless subjects. People sit for days in airless conference rooms building their mission statements, learning the not-so-subtle distinctions of sexual harassment and re-engineering their departments. Your flip charts may be fantastic, your slides colorful, and your video displays brilliant, but a picture of a fire is not a fire. Unless there is a real fire inside of you, your presentation may be technically correct but humanly inadequate. No matter how grandly your topic is chosen and prepared, if you are out of touch with your own passion, impact will elude you. You don't have to be a raging bonfire—a single candle flame will do. It's when you bring this flame into the mundane and the repetitive that serious problems get lightened, and everyone starts having fun!

Passion is not about being perfect! It's about being alive!
Speaking is not about being perfect! It's about passion!

So brother,
if you *still* got to ask
what all this jazz is about—
you probably ain't got it.
There's a lot of the jazz musician
in every speaker of impact.

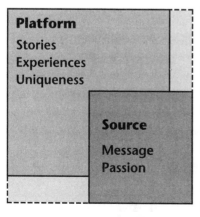

Audiences have windows: They have *platforms* that they show the public; they have *masks* that keep their images in place; there are the *blind spots* they think no one sees; and they have *sources* where real passion and energy can be touched. As a speaker, you connect your window to theirs. You meet with each other on the platform, but impact happens at the source.

WHAT AUDIENCES HEAR AND REMEMBER

Finding the Fit with Diverse Audiences

We somehow assume
That because we say it
In words, generally understood
That they get it.

So are seldom aware of
What we are really communicating.

The newspaper headline read, "Mars More than a Ball of Rock," and the ensuing article revealed three things a planet needs to just possibly be hospitable to life: a crust, an inner mantle, and a core. It reported that since Mars holds these properties, there's the possibility that life might have been there once . . . which brings us to audiences!

As we search the planets for signs of life, so speakers search the faces of audiences for discernible signs. Audiences also possess the three planetary life possibilities: crust, that outer face (their platform); a hidden mantle (their masks and blinders); and a core (their source). Every speaker knows that behind each face is an invisible "on/off" switch, and the challenge is to find the "on" switch!

Guarding every person's "on" switch is a unique filtering system that can be pictured as an open umbrella with tiny holes that let the world in or keep it out. Billboard images, television repetition, freeway gridlock, noise, speakers—all rain down on this filter umbrella. To know an audience is to know what gets through their filter, what flips their "on" switch.

Learning style researchers, beginning with Carl Jung and extending to educators Fisher, Gregoric, Merrill, and McCarthy have all contributed to a similar model of how people learn. I've always viewed this model as an excellent resource for the speaker–audience relationship, and to my knowledge it has not been so translated until now. Step back and view this model from the larger perspective of what audiences hear and remember.

WHAT AUDIENCES HEAR

People hear what they want to hear, what fits their belief system and sustains their life structure. Picture a vertical line with the words *Concrete* at the top and *Abstract* at the bottom. Everyone's "on" switch is somewhere on this line.

Concrete People

I remember stepping into an elevator one morning at what was then the Adams Hotel in Phoenix, Arizona, and being greeted by a large, courtly man with a huge cigar. I was conducting a series of seminars at the hotel for the National Association of Bank Women, and we women were totally outnumbered by a hotel full of conventioneers from the Cement Industry. Huge banners draped the lobby welcoming everyone to "The Wonderful World of Cement," and, as I stepped into the elevator that morning, this gracious and benevolent gentleman extended to me probably the only option he could think of for a woman encased in this assemblage of men. He smiled down at me over the tip of his cigar and charitably asked,

"Is your husband in cement?"

What a one liner!! Especially because I was from Chicago (Chicago . . . Bang, Bang . . .).

Comfortable in Cement

Some people are comfortable in cement. They like their information to be concrete, real, and tangible. They want to talk about actual events as opposed to hypothetical situations. They like specific examples and clear categories that tell them exactly where they are going. These people will give you feedback like this:

- "Tell me what to do, and I'll do it!"
- "Don't read me the book; just tell me what I need right now."
- "I like a speaker to have clear points and stick to them."

Concrete people don't want you to dump a lot of separate pieces in their lap; they'd rather you put everything together, pour the mix, and give them the results. They want their information and experiences to be explicit and tangible: A person should say what he or she means, a speech should sound like a speech, and speakers should tell them what they're going to hear and how they are personally involved. Don't load them down with information they're not going use, just give the essentials. They're comfortable involving their senses; when presented with new situations, they rely on their feelings first. They like to be a part of the experience, to have an idea presented so graphically that they can touch it, see it, hear it, smell it! They're sitting on the front rows so as not to miss anything.

Abstract People

At the other end of this vertical line are the people who like to keep some distance from the information and experiences that enter their lives. "To abstract" is to draw away, to separate from the actual physical moment. These people easily retreat into their minds, to logic, reason, and inner observation. They are good at detaching and often talk about situations and people without directly referencing them. They love discussions that separate them from daily routine and take them into possibilities. People who are abstractors may retreat from the real world to the ideal, and, as the author and psychologist William James once described, "They shed tears over injustice and inequality and may not see these qualities when they meet them in the street." People who are comfortable in a more abstract place will say to you:

- ■ "If I wanted a condensation, I'd read the dictionary."
- ■ "Don't tell me your answer, I want to figure it out for myself!"
- ■ "Please, leave something to my imagination!"
- ■ "I like a speaker who gives me the facts and lets me draw my own conclusions."

They listen for logical sequencing of causes/effects, theoretical information, and the introduction of possibilities. They want enough information to determine for themselves what is important; they often resent being told what they're going to hear—they'll recognize it themselves. They're organized, exacting, and objective; if a speaker gets emotional, they prefer that it be structured and not get too close.

All Hear What They Want to Hear

Each person and each audience is a combination of the concrete and the abstract. It's up to the speaker to weave the right blend so that each person will "hear you"! Here are some suggestions for adapting your content and style to build that balance.

HOW TO CONNECT

With the Concrete People in Audiences	With the Abstract People in Audiences
1. Begin with a solid opening.	
■ *Grab their attention* with a question that hits home, a shocking statement, unbelievable information, an opening that brings them straight up in their chairs.	■ *Attract their attention; don't grab.* It's a matter of touch—you can use that shocker but take them quickly out of it.
■ *In their face!* Don't be afraid of closeups; they prefer head shots to scenery. Zoom in, and let them see expressions; hook them with an enlargement of a specific.	■ *Long shots!* These folks feel safer with some distance. They like reference to the big picture and the overview.

With the Concrete People in Audiences	**With the Abstract People in Audiences**
2. Involve their senses!	
▪ Invite them to touch, see, hear, smell.	▪ Emphasize the visual, auditory.
▪ Involve them physically and emotionally.	▪ Involve them mentally and don't force it.
3. Talk to them as people.	
▪ Talk about specific feelings, experiences.	▪ Talk about mind, logic, reason.
▪ Use real situations, people, examples.	▪ Use hypothetical examples and other people's situations.
4. Give them the big picture.	
▪ Start with how the audience fits into the big picture.	▪ Start with visualizing the big picture.
▪ Connect each point to the larger picture.	▪ Move to the specific parts (points).
▪ Tell them what each means.	▪ Suggest meanings, give time to consider.
▪ Move the group to decision and action.	▪ Challenge them to find their own meaning.
5. Keep everything moving.	
▪ Use a lot of action.	▪ Use enough action to keep the content alive.
▪ Keep them personally with you.	▪ Keep them mentally with you.
▪ Round numbers to the nearest whole.	▪ Give the exact figures.
▪ Be concise, give the short version.	▪ Give access to more than the short version.
▪ Give short descriptions.	▪ Give details, just don't bore them.

HOW TO PROJECT CREDIBILITY

With the Concrete People in Audiences	With the Abstract People in Audiences
■ Be an expert on your *topic*. ■ Communicate your *experience* with this topic area to the audience.	■ Expand beyond topic to the entire *field*. ■ Communicate your *credentials* to the audience.

HOW TO PROVIDE SUBSTANCE

With the Concrete People in Audiences	With the Abstract People in Audiences

1. Say something important.

■ Say what's important to them *personally*. ■ Back it up with specifics. ■ Be the voice of *experience*.	■ Say what's of *practical* importance to them. ■ Be prepared to stand behind what you say. ■ Be the voice of *authority*.

2. Give answers, solutions, tips.

■ Make them short and specific. ■ Make them easy and possible to do now. ■ Show the personal benefits. ■ Show how to proceed, step-by-step.	■ Make them logical and specific. ■ Give the details, perhaps in a handout. ■ Show the logical, practical benefits. ■ Identify results, present guidelines.

3. Open a new perspective.

■ Appeal to their *experience*. ■ Open them to new *ways*. ■ *Picture* for them this new perspective.	■ Appeal to their *logical* side. ■ Open them to new *possibilities*. ■ *Challenge* them to find a new perspective.

HOW TO *CUSTOMIZE*

With the Concrete People in Audiences	With the Abstract People in Audiences
1. Know them personally.	
▪ Know their names and experiences.	▪ Know their names and titles.
▪ Know how they feel and empathize with them.	▪ Know how they think and what they align with.
2. Know their industry.	
▪ Know their problems and their pain.	▪ Know their acronyms and issues.
▪ Acknowledge their pain and problems.	▪ Acknowledge their progress.
▪ Tell them about people in other industries.	▪ Tell them about what worked in other systems.
▪ Know enough of their history for perspective.	▪ Know their history for specifics.

A QUICK REVIEW

Concrete Audiences Hear	Abstract Audiences Hear
Big picture	Individual parts
Short descriptions	Complete descriptions
Distinct categories	Shades of possibilities
All-inclusive instructions	End results leave the method open
Whatever is tangible	
Summaries	Hypothetical
A quick read	The whole script
Concrete experience	Intricate "who done it"
Numbers rounded off to the nearest whole	Experiences of others
	The exact figures
Actual situations	Theoretical models
Certainty	Paradox

With *Concrete* Audiences	With *Abstract* Audiences
1. Come from your own experience and feelings. Use real people and situations that the audience has experienced.	1. Base your talk on a factual, logical premise. Use hypothetical examples. They are comfortable "in theory" and enjoy grappling with paradoxes.
2. Condense data and don't overburden them with details. Tell them what they need and how to do it.	2. Give enough data/detail for them to find their own meaning, possible connections, and solutions.
3. Speak from knowledge with empathy.	3. Speak with authority.

Note: There's the old saying "You can't win them all" but I find that when a speaker consciously works with a blend of both approaches, everyone gets something and impact is stronger.

WHAT AUDIENCES REMEMBER

People remember what they experience either actively or thoughtfully. To avoid the tendency of "in one ear and out the other," the speaker must know something of how people in the audience process information, how they best learn, understand, and solve problems. How does the speaker enhance the remembering process of both active and reflective people in an audience? Here are some suggestions.

Picture a horizontal line—with the words *action* at the far left and *reflection* at the far right. As we place people along this line, we'll build the impact blend.

Action ←————→ **Reflection**

HOW ACTION PEOPLE PROCESS INFORMATION: HANDS ON, EXPERIMENTATION

When my "heartson" Dylan was growing up, I would go to the junkyard and look for a mangled object that had a lot of intricate parts. After making sure that the chosen object was basically safe, I'd wrap it up in a great box and add it to the gifts under the tree at holiday time. On Christmas morning, he'd dive into this huge, intriguing crate, pull out the hulking object (the bigger the better), drag it out to the back yard, and proceed to take it apart. What a great exploration! He could smash it, stomp on it, take wire cutters and dismantle it, but most important he could figure out what it was, what was wrong, and maybe even how to fix it!

A lot of grown men and women have this same zest when they unwrap a problem that needs solving or a project that needs definition. These are *action* people. They gladly lug home huge "self-assembly" boxes and happily work their way through all the complex parts. They love the challenge of figuring things out for themselves. They will say to you:

- ▪ "Let me try it!"
- ▪ "If I can tinker with it a bit, I'll figure it out."
- ▪ "Talk, talk, talk! Let's get going."
- ▪ "I like a speaker who gets right into it, who doesn't waste time telling me what I can find out for myself."

They may sit through hours of briefings, but it only makes sense when they can try it themselves; an explanation doesn't register unless they can simultaneously be exploring it. These people must have physical contact; they will remember only what they handle themselves, and as long as they have this hands-on experience, they stay involved.

People who learn through action are often guilty of "Ready, *fire*, aim!" They jump into the middle of lakes and learn to swim their way back to shore. Planning and organizing are often not their strong points, because it takes too much time, and they are more accurate working from the center of the action. These common-sense people who learn best by practice and repetition have very little patience with slow starters. They like speakers who get right to the point, who use action language and keep an energetic pace. They want a speaker to have a direction and get there! They are practical nuts-and-bolts folks. If it doesn't work, get rid of it. This same attitude carries over to the speakers they listen to.

HOW REFLECTIVE PEOPLE PROCESS INFORMATION: OBSERVE AND THINK ABOUT IT

Reflective audiences are not the guys who race down the pier and plunge headfirst into the water. They will walk to the end of the dock, examine the water, double-check the depth, and focus their courage for a cautious (though perfect) dive. Reflective people like to start with an idea and take some time to think about it. They study life through questionnaires and reflect on what they find.

They will say to you:

- "I'd like to sleep on it for a while before making my decision."
- "Just leave me alone for now; let me get it straight in my mind."
- "I'll think on it and let you know."
- "Don't rush me!"
- "If you give me a little time, I'm sure I can come up with a use for this."
- "Let me program it into my head, and I'll probably get an answer in the middle of the night."

They start with what they see and generalize. They like a speaker who begins from a specific point of view and opens them up to a larger reality. They like a speaker who doesn't repeat what others say, but who has made his or her own studies and has a contribution of a new information and insight. In designing your talk for reflective people, never push them to assimilate important material too quickly. Introduce and return; give time for thinking and getting comfortable.

ALL REMEMBER WHAT IMPACTS THEM

Whether active or reflective, the *three levels of impact* discussed in Chapter 1 still apply:

- Level one: The audience hears you; what audiences hear.
- Level two: The audience gets it—the "Ahaa"; what audiences remember.
- Level three: The audience takes action; what audiences do.

What can the speaker do to bring an audience to the second and third levels of impact? What moves can a speaker make to enhance the process of *both* active and reflective audiences? Here are some suggestions.

Give *action* audiences:

1. Hands-on involvement.
   - Structure a talk as a progressive story where the audience comes along with you.
   - Stay in the present tense.
   - Whenever you want an idea to stick, attach it to some action.
   - Pace your talk so there is some action every few minutes (depending on the group's attention span).

2. Experimentation.
   - An attitude of "let's try it and see" sets the challenge.
   - Reward the effort.
3. Repetition.
   - Repetition of an action increases its holding power.
   - Be careful not to give repetition to mistakes.
   - Explore ways to repeat an idea in both concrete and abstract terms.

Give *reflective* audiences:

1. Observation.
   - Give observation breaks, within your material.
   - Let them observe themselves: video, group feedback, assessment tools.
   - Let them observe each other: role play, group contribution, video.
   - Ask them to reflect on their own experiences.
   - Break an idea into parts and let them move with you into observation of each part.
2. Research.
   - Set up an immediate mental challenge.
   - Challenge the amateur sleuths; give clues along the way.
   - Give enough description to set their minds working.
   - Give reflective distance: introduce a point, move on to something else, then come back to it.
   - Put ideas/points into rational categories, let the audience help you classify.
3. Possibilities.
   - Carefully develop a concept throughout your talk, using repetition and audience involvement to anchor it in their minds.
   - What if? Suppose you were the decision maker, what are the possibilities?

An anchor holds a ship in place—because there's a hook that digs in and won't let go! This is what we want to anchor with the audience: a hook that they can't forget, one that takes them to impact. As speakers, we address four different preferences in audiences: the concrete and the abstract listeners; the active and reflective recallers. We're now ready to put them together and identify the four faces in every audience.

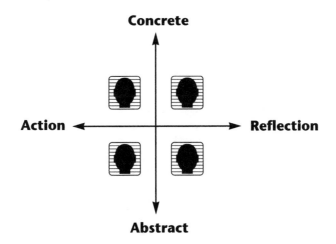

Concrete

Action ◄————————————► **Reflection**

Abstract

THE FOUR FACES IN EVERY AUDIENCE

Connecting with Each

Every audience has its own energy
Its own personality.
No two audiences are ever the same.
No single audience is ever the same again.
Each has a signature
A pulse
A face of its own!
Ah, what surprises lie behind a face?

*We buy a ticket to Gilbert and Sullivan and
when we get to the theater,
we find it's Arnold Schwarzenegger.*

Speakers know about looking out into a sea of faces! There are
the smiling faces that nod approval and the faces that glow;
there are the serious faces with frozen expressions; the blur of
faces at the back of the room; and the faces that never look
up. Faces mirror behavior! There are the eager front-row
attentives, the volunteers, the talkers, and the expressionless
ones. Some faces flash "relationship"; others say "data." How
do we connect with every face?

- How do we get more comfortable facing faces?
- How do we keep from focusing on the one face that isn't
  buying?
- How do we bring one message to each face?

Figure 7.1

The Four Faces in an Audience

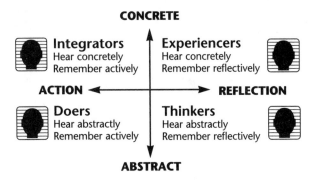

CONCRETE

Integrators Hear concretely Remember actively	**Experiencers** Hear concretely Remember reflectively

ACTION ←————————→ REFLECTION

Doers Hear abstractly Remember actively	**Thinkers** Hear abstractly Remember reflectively

ABSTRACT

We've looked at the spread between *concrete* and *abstract* communication. We've walked the line between *active* and *reflective* reinforcement. Now it's time to cross the lines and construct the *four faces* in an audience: the experiencers, the thinkers, the doers, and the integrators (see Figure 7.1).

The Face of the Experiencer

Let your own experience be a stepping-stone for working with the world.

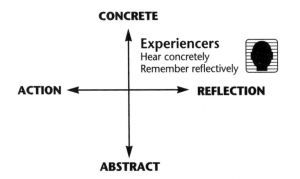

CONCRETE

Experiencers
Hear concretely
Remember reflectively

ACTION ←————————→ REFLECTION

ABSTRACT

They hear concretely; they learn and remember reflectively

What They Hear	What They Want	Where They're Good
■ People concerns ■ Big picture; the whole ■ Personal meaning ■ What they can feel, touch, smell, hear, and taste ■ Other people's emotions	■ To know *"who?"* ■ To know *"why?"* ■ To enter into an experience ■ To integrate personal meaning ■ "What's the learning for me?" ■ To express their emotions	■ Person-to-person ■ Analysis ■ Observation and reflection ■ Listening and contributing ■ Pulling together diverse elements and entering into it ■ Imagination, innovation ■ Brainstorming, discussion

At the Monterey Language School in California, I presented a two-week training session to the language instructors. On the first day, they presented me with a huge flowchart of the entire support organization and defined where they did and didn't fit in. Expressing deep concern for their students, they were active participants, talking frankly about their experiences and insightfully identified problems in both their own behaviors and those of their bosses. Warm, friendly, conscientious, bright, and all experts in their own fields, they quickly became a cohesive team, role playing and contributing to discussions. At the close of the session, they individually thanked me for an experience that had application to their personal lives. When I left, they presented me with a huge, handmade card containing everyone's handwritten message and a color drawing of me driving away in my car with all of them standing around waving good-bye.

These people were *experiencers*. They wanted me to create an experience for them where they could reflect and integrate their whole person. When one person would tell his or her story, everyone would step into the same story and identify how much they all had in common.

Experiencers are often called "feelers" because they tactually and emotionally feel their way along to right decisions. They need to touch the situation, actually drive to the site, go through the records themselves, feel themselves in the same dilemma. Only when they are personally connected can they make next-step decisions.

These are "people people" who hear the world through empathetic ears. In any crisis or situation, they want to know how *people* are affected, what others are doing and feeling, who they talk to, and what they say. Wherever the camera goes, they want to see the faces of the people, and they definitely want their own face to be in the picture.

Big picture is preferable to the smaller details. They want to know *why* things happen, how they all connect, and what is the concrete *reason* behind actions. Because they perceive through their senses and their emotions, their feelings must be recognized, validated, and expressed. They want to be touched and to touch. The late Princess Di spoke to a world audience through her "touch."

Who Are the Experiencers?
- People who work with and are good with children.
- People who study life and reflect on their findings.
- People who get their satisfaction from making a difference.
- People who talk about their feelings.
- People who use the verb *feel* a lot: i.e., "I *feel* it is important," "How can you *feel* good about that job?" "It *feels* right to me!"
- People who draw every conversation to themselves: i.e., when you lead with a statement like, "A city bus hit my car this morning," and the immediate response is, "I know how you feel, the same thing happened to me," you know you're talking to an *experiencer*.

Most of us have some experiencer inside of us, but here are some groups who tend to wear this face more predictably.

- Charity workers
- Children
- Government employees
- Health care workers
- Human resource people
- Human services workers
- Meeting planners
- Organizational development groups
- Parents groups
- Social scientists
- Supervisors
- Teachers
- Volunteers
- Women's groups

It's a pretty safe bet that these groups are strongly composed of *experiencers*.

Where *Experiencers* Are Strong

1. They have excellent *people skills;* they listen, observe, and have empathy.
2. They're good at *analysis;* their natural inclination to reflect on what they see happening is an excellent basis for pulling diverse elements together.
3. They're strong *contributors.* Many times *experiencers* hear themselves by talking something through. They usually have an opinion and are only too glad to voice it.
4. They come up with *creative solutions.* Role playing and brainstorming can get really innovative; imagination is an attribute.

Tips for Connecting with *Experiencers*

Words
- Use tactile words and expressions.
- Use the verb "to feel."

Speaking Style:
- Let them see your feelings.
- Use a more personal, less formal style.

- Be interactive.
- Take them there; don't just tell them about it.
- Find a way for them to express their emotions.
- Define your process early.
- Encourage their participation.

Content
- Talk about people; if there is no people component, they won't be interested.
- Give reasons *why* it is important.
- Use observation and analysis.
- Relate everything to them.
- Be creative.
- Give more weight to people's reactions than to dollar amounts and impersonal results.
- Find the human angle.
- Opinions are as important as facts.

The Speaker's Role
- Be a motivator.
- Set up an environment for them to experience.

The Face of the Thinker

How do I work? I grope!

Albert Einstein

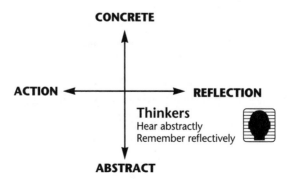

They hear abstractly; They learn and remember reflectively

What They Hear	What They Want	Where They're Good
■ Intellectual approaches	■ To be taught	■ Analysis; what's happening
■ Reason and logic	■ Facts	■ Concept development
■ Theoretical models	■ Information	■ Reflecting on the experiences of others
■ Systematic methods	■ To know *what*	
■ Goals	■ To examine the experience from the outside	■ Abstract conceptualization
■ Sequenced organization	■ Structured emotional climate	■ Comparing relationships
■ Objectivity	■ To make their own decisions	■ Close examination of small pieces of information
■ Exacting material		■ Objectivity

Thinkers want the speaker to present them with the big picture and then to break it into smaller components. They want you to do your homework and come with all the necessary information. They want hard facts, exacting and sourced; credibility and accuracy are critical.

Though highly emotional people, their passion is directed to preciseness, sound reason, and logical conclusions. Feelings are often not in their vocabulary and are experienced only within controlled activities. They are rigorous about tracing a problem to its source, devising systematic approaches, and integrating their findings. They like presenters who display a linear organization, sequence their points, and get enthusiastic over conceptual ideas.

They want to know *what* is going on here! What are the details they should be aware of, what is the latest research, and exactly how much will it cost? They want time to think about what they are hearing and to mentally examine the ideas. Though they want solutions to solve problems, they are comfortable living with the problem or the puzzle until they can sort it out.

A reasonable impact level to target with these audiences is that they hear you (Level 1, Chapter 1) and that they get something tangible to think on. The "Ahaa" (Level 2, Chapter 1) may come to them days later.

Who Are the *Thinkers*?
- People who love to solve problems.
- Crossword puzzle addicts.
- People who analyze a lot.
- People who solve big problems one step at a time.
- People who really like detail work.
- People who want things classified and in their proper place.
- People who must find a rational explanation.
- People who put high value on credentials, titles, and prior experience.

Again, it is hoped that we all have some thinker inside of us; however, there are some groups and professions that tend to draw them:

- Accountants
- Administrators
- Anthropologists
- Astrologers
- Auditors
- Doctors, dentists
- Engineers
- Historians
- Library science workers
- Managers
- Mathematicians
- Philosophers
- Professors
- Researchers
- Technicians
- Writers

Where Are Thinkers Strong?

1. *They catch the mistakes.* Their expertise for accuracy and exactness carries over into observation and analysis. They see small details that are often missed, incongruencies that can get overlooked.
2. *They have patience.* They can start with an idea, reflect on it, play around with it, and watch it take shape. At some point, they put the picture together, see the connections, and devise appropriate action.
3. *They are direct thinkers.* They arrange what happens and what they perceive into rational categories. After making a judgment, they usually review and then monitor the accuracy of that decision.
4. *They are objective.*
5. *They are great problem solvers.* Observation, analysis, classification, and conclusions are all strengths.

Tips for Connecting with Thinkers

Words

- Use rational, objective words.
- Stay away from "feel."

Speaking Style

- Be enthusiastic but not personally emotional.
- Speak as the authority.
- Don't try too hard; relax.
- Some interaction is fine but not immediately.
- Be as visual as possible.
- Be organized, systematic, and logical.
- Use hypothetical examples.
- Encourage but don't insist on participation.

Content

- Talk about ideas, concepts, systems, methods, organizations, results.
- Give the facts and the exact figures.

■ Answer the *what* questions:
- • What is the situation?
- • What are the causes?
- • What has been done thus far?
- • What are the desired results?
- • What is the prognosis?

The Speaker's Role
■ Teach them.
■ Be a witness to their own observations.

The Face of the Doer

Perspective becomes action.

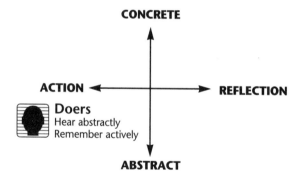

They hear abstractly; They learn and remember actively

What They Hear	What They Want	Where They're Good
■ Practical applications ■ Common sense ■ Physical action ■ Specific directions	■ To know *how* things work ■ A single answer ■ To solve the problem ■ To test it themselves	■ Making things work ■ Exploration ■ Following directions ■ Experimentation

Doers want less talk and more action; they want a speaker to keep them moving. Though they have a strong ability to focus on projects, their listening attention span can be short. They're the ones that take repeated trips to the bathroom during your talk, who fidget in their seats and doze off on you. They need to be actively *doing* something.

These are usually down-to-earth folks who respect plain talk, an honest try, and ordinary people. They use their body senses for understanding. They'll respect experience over a college degree; who you are and what you've done are all they need to know. They're good at seeing through pretense and hype; they are good judges of character and are quick to size up people and put them in convenient categories. Making their goal turns them on! They love to solve the problem, get to the destination, and finish the job! These are the people that you want around if your life is in danger, because they'll get you to safety; they often take professions and occupations that involve crisis action. They're innovative, they'll use anything and everything to make their goal!

Who Are the *Doers*?

- The people who get the job done.
- People who can fix anything.
- People who find a way, no matter how little there is to go on.
- People who love a physical challenge.
- Knights in shining armor who ride white horses.
- Crisis addicts; if there isn't a crisis, they'll make one.
- People who have to keep busy.

Thinkers often cross over this line, but here are some groups that are known for the ability to *do*.

- Agricultural workers
- Ambulance drivers
- Architects
- Artists
- Athletes
- Coaches
- Contractors
- Craftspeople
- Crisis and command center people
- Engineers
- Fire fighters
- Inventors
- Maintenance people
- Musicians
- Physical scientists
- Police
- Repair people
- Service industry people
- Supervisors
- Testers
- Tradespeople and union-members
- Trouble shooters

Where Are Doers Strong?

1. *Following directions.* They build on the givens and can organize information.
2. *Deductive reasoning.* They start with what they know and work from there.
3. *Improvising.* They're masterfully creative when it comes to making do with what they have and finding what they need.
4. *Practical applications.* Their major question is, "What can this be used for?" and they find uses for everything.
5. *Problem solving.*
6. *Getting the job done and making things work.*
7. *Doing the impossible.*

Tips for Connecting with Doers

Words

- Use functional terminology.
- Speak in plain talk.

Speaking Style
- Be practical.
- Avoid airs; be who you are.
- Take small steps to small successes.
- Retreat from possible failure.
- Be interactive.
- Lead them to discover for themselves.
- Use common sense.

Content
- Use worksheets—they feel safe.
- Keep it simple and systematic.
- Make practical applications.
- Things are safer than people.
- Focus; follow one route at a time.
- Look for a definite, single, correct solution.
- Speak to their primary interest, *"how?"*

The Speaker's Role
- Plan and implement the experience, discussion, or analysis.
- Encourage and acknowledge successes.
- Move them on to new approaches.

The Face of the Integrator

Consistency is the last refuge of the unimaginative.

Oscar Wilde

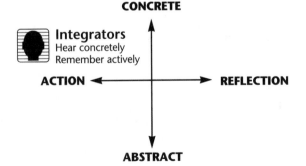

They hear concretely; They learn and remember actively

What They Hear	What They Want	Where They're Good
▪ Concrete experience ▪ Knowledge combined with personal experience and experimentation ▪ What the experts say ▪ Possibilities ▪ New ways	▪ Integration of information ▪ To enrich reality ▪ To learn on their own ▪ To make something better ▪ Their major questions are: •What can this become? •What can I make of this?	▪ Adapting ▪ Intuitive; trial-and-error ▪ At ease with people ▪ Self-discovery ▪ Rely on other people for information

Integrators are never satisfied; they're always looking to the next project and the next challenge. Something can always be done differently or better. They hire the futurist to speak to them about what's ahead; they are especially keen on hearing new perspectives and new ways to organize and implement.

Who Are the Integrators?

▪ These are the people who listen to the experts but check it out for themselves.

▪ The minute something works, they are trying to figure out how to make it better.

▪ They are the collectors and the information gatherers.

▪ They hear an idea and immediately see ten possibilities for it.

▪ They break a dish and turn the shards into an art piece.

▪ They don't throw it away because they'll find a use for it.

▪ They can turn unbelievably unlikely arrays into a marvelous unity.

▪ They figure things out for themselves and share with others.

Here are some groups where you will find integrators.

- Advertising people
- Designers
- Directors
- Entrepreneurs
- Idea people
- Inventors
- Leaders
- Mediators
- Managers
- Planners
- Politicians
- Real estate people
- Restaurant and fast-food industry workers
- Sales and marketing people
- Think-tank members
- Travel agents
- Web designers

Where Are Integrators Strong?

1. They are self-starters and self-challengers.
2. They are big-picture people and immediately see the interconnections.
3. They are highly adaptable and make use of everything around them.
4. They are intuitive, not afraid of mistakes; their process is usually trial-and-error.
5. They're tuned into self-discovery and learn from their experiences.
6. They're usually at ease with people and communicate well.
7. Perhaps their greatest skill is integration, their ability to bring odd pieces together and find the fit.

Tips for Connecting with Integrators

Words

- Use functional terminology.
- Speak in plain talk.

Speaking Style

- Be wild and creative.
- Start anywhere.
- Take it where it goes.
- Be colorful.
- Take a risk.
- Be interactive.

Content

- Use concrete experiences.
- Talk about possibilities and new ways.
- Recycle the present into the future.
- Choose topics that involve people.
- Openly refer to and use intuition.
- Stress applications and usefulness.

The Speaker's Role

- Challenge, encourage, guide, and reinforce.
- Start with what they see, hear, touch, feel.
- Let them try it out or intuit results.
- Guide them in their decisions.

Each person in the audience is a combination of two or more faces, but most have a primary face. The speaker of impact develops the expertise of connecting with each face, talking in terms each can understand, adapting content, style, and process to maximize each connection. This art of alignment becomes an integral part of your platform skill. You learn to cover all four bases in every talk:

1. To the Experiencers, you relate content to the audience.
2. To the Thinkers, you give the details, the facts.
3. To the Doers, you show how it works, how it is practical.
4. To the Integrators, you take it to possibilities.

In so doing, everyone's vision expands and you connect with every audience.

Figure 7.2

The Speaker's Platform Connects with Each Face

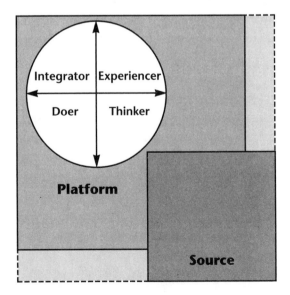

THE SPEAKER
MAKES IT SAFE

Sticks and stones
Can break your bones
But words
Can never hurt you.

Says who?

We learned the illusion of safety early. Perhaps it was when
we first made it to daddy's arms without falling down that we
found we could do it, and someone was there to catch us!
Later in life we took this illusion of safety to a higher level:
Airplanes crash, but not the one we're flying; other people get
fired, but our job is safe; and of course—everyone else gets
wrinkles. We live with these small denials just fine, and,
when they don't work, we just close our eyes and don't look.
I call this "not looking" strategy the "cat and rat camouflage."

When my great hunter, Mr. Cat, would bring me a dead
trophy and lay it on the deck, I first would have to cover it
with a newspaper before I could deal with it and then only
very judiciously with a long-handled shovel. I just couldn't
look at it. There are a lot of things audiences don't want to
look at and safe means not being forced to look at what you
can't or don't want to handle. Sometimes the speaker has to
lay a little newspaper and provide some covering in order to
proceed. When audiences trust that no dead rats will be laid

out on the deck, no one will be put on the spot, coerced, embarrassed, or made wrong, then the scene can be set for impact.

There came a time when I could deal more directly with the reality of "rat," and I dispensed with the newspaper. As the speaker reinforces an environment of protection and respect, audiences remove their coverings and deal more directly with their fears. This is the path to impact!

SPEAKER SAFETY

A frightened captain makes for a frightened crew.

■ A jittery driver is a menace on the road.
■ A supervisor who is scared of his or her boss passes that fear on to workers.
■ A dentist whose hand shakes does not instill confidence.

A speaker who is uncertain and tries too hard will communicate the message of "unsafe." It's imperative that you, the speaker, feel comfortable with the situation and with the audience. Let's look at what this involves.

The Situation

What helps you, the speaker, feel more comfortable (safe)?

■ *Room size.* What size room are you most comfortable working in?
■ *Category.* Do you prefer keynotes, after dinner talks, panels, team speaking, or training?
■ *Position.* Do you prefer to be the feature speaker, the adjunct speaker, or to speak in concurrent sessions?
■ *Length.* Are you more comfortable at up to one hour, one to three hours, three to six hours, or more?

■ *Style.* Do you prefer formal, informal, or casual?

■ *Structure.* Are you more comfortable with a fully scripted presentation, controlled interaction, improvisation, or open question/answers?

What Makes You, the Speaker, Feel "Unsafe"?

Do you have trouble handling any of these situations?

A last-minute change in the program:
■ A room change.
■ A sudden change in speaking order.
■ A last-minute addition.

You have the wrong information:
■ You discover a hidden agenda.
■ Essential information has been withheld.
■ You've talked to the wrong people.

You are without materials:
■ Your materials don't arrive.
■ You grabbed the wrong handouts.
■ You brought the wrong visuals.

Suddenly you go blank:
■ You are distracted by something in the room.
■ You totally forget where you are in your talk.
■ You pull a total blank.

Your speaking time is changed:
■ A late start requires you to cut your talk.
■ The business meeting before the speech runs long.
■ You suddenly have more time than you planned.

Suddenly you have to wing it:
- An off-the-wall question comes from the audience.
- You have to make a last-minute content switch.
- You suddenly have to add something new.

Technically something goes wrong:
- There's a power failure—the lights go out.
- There is no microphone at the last moment.
- There are audio-visual failures.

An accident occurs:
- Something happens to someone in the audience.
- All your notes and materials get confused.
- Something rips or shows that's not supposed to.

How do you handle these emergencies? Know you own strategies for emergency safety.

Notes for Your Emergency Safety Strategy

_____

_____

_____

_____

_____

Learning from Tough Situations

Experience is a great teacher! Whenever you have a really tough talk time, do some "Monday morning quarterbacking," and get clear on two items: (1) What was unsafe for you in that situation? (2) What did you learn about making the situation safe for yourself? I'll lead with one of the toughest situations I ever encountered.

I once discovered at the last minute that the audience expected something completely different from what I was prepared to deliver. The speaking engagement had been contracted through a major university in another country with all communication translated through the university office and I was never allowed to speak directly to the client. When I realized that the client wanted cut-throat negotiation techniques instead of management skills, I dumped three solid days of preparation to wing it with "swimming with the sharks."

What Made Me Feel Unsafe
Having to wing it without preparation, supporting materials, or visuals.

What I Learned
1. Never take an assignment, no matter how attractive, without directly interfacing with the client. Personally make sure that all information is accurate and complete. Sometimes it's your intuition that has to read between the lines of what they say and what they mean.
2. Always bring backup materials on related subjects, just in case an audience question or a surprise need calls for further documentation. I always think, "What could go wrong?" and prepare for eventualities, especially the ones that make me feel unsafe.

What Is Your Tough Speaking Situation?

Situation: _____

_____

_____

What made it "unsafe"? _____

_____

_____

_____

How would you handle it again? _____

_____

_____

_____

This is important information to know about yourself. Your responsibility as a speaker is to create a situation that offers the best opportunity for impact. To do this, it's important to know: (1) what you need for safety; and (2) how to build a safety net.

THE AUDIENCE

With What Audiences Do You Feel Most Safe?

Some audiences feel like family; others feel like aliens. Think about the audiences with whom you do your best work; is there a profile identifying the people you are most effective with?

- Gender diversity: All women, all men, a mix?
- Age diversity: Children, teens, college, young adults, older adults, seniors, a mix?
- Professional diversity: White collar, blue collar, or a mix?
- Racial/ethnic diversity: Is there a particular race or ethnic group with whom you are really at home? Do you prefer a racial or ethnic mix within your audience?

Audience Responses That Can Throw a Speaker into "Unsafe"

Do any of these audience responses cause you to feel unsafe?

- Someone doesn't look at you; one person is looking down or away, never giving eye contact.
- No response; poker face, no smile, no head nod, no laugh.
- Competition; a conversation in the audience while you are speaking.
- Audience attention goes elsewhere; one or more people are doing something else such as subtly reading a newspaper or writing.
- No questions; you ask for questions, and no one speaks up.
- People in and out; bathroom and smoke breaks, people slipping out at the back of the room.

Learning from Tough Responses

Even experienced speakers have their tough audiences. Here was one of mine:

> A group of forest service men in one of our more remote areas of our national forests sat for two hours looking at the floor and spitting "chew" into styrofoam cups. When my stress level got so high I couldn't take it anymore, I stopped midsentence, sat down in a chair, took a long drink of water from a *clean* styrofoam cup, and said, "You know, I really want to talk with you, but I just can't do it when nobody looks at me. What's wrong?" There was total silence. Finally one man in the back mumbled that he didn't want to be here, and all the heads nodded. It took another hour of "just talking together" before it was safe enough to return to my talk. When we did, everyone got involved.

What Felt "Unsafe"

A low-energy audience who refused to look at me and connect with the topic.

What I Learned

Deal with the problem immediately!

Your Tough Audience Response

What about the audiences who have been hard for you to connect with? Recall a really tough response, look at what made you feel unsafe, and how you would handle it now.

Situation: _____

_____

_____

What Felt Unsafe? _____

_____

_____

How Would You Handle It Now? _____

_____

_____

BUILD SPEAKER SAFETY NETS

First: Set Yourself Up for Success

Make every effort to secure a physical setup that feels safe and comfortable for you—where you do your best work. Learn to ask for what you need and to say no to obvious setups for trouble. A friend of mine and colleague, Gloria Hutter, was asked to speak to a travel association on her area of expertise,

"Business Etiquette." The meeting place was at one of San Francisco's well-known enjoyment centers that Gloria described as a noise factory with drinks and food—fun for participants but trouble for a speaker. She said to them, "I'm very sorry, but the room doesn't fit my image, and my message will not come across; please invite me again when you meet in at a different place." A few months later she spoke to them at the Ritz Carlton Hotel.

Second: Expand Your Flexibility

If large audiences frighten you, take one on where other safety factors can be managed, such as with familiar people, perhaps in an informal setting. If you're a trainer and used to full-day sessions, do some short talks that force you to refine. If speaking auditions terrify you, make yourself do as many as possible. Continually expand your own experience of "safe." When certain audience responses tend to throw you off balance, welcome them, and ask other speakers how they handle similar situations. Every tough audience response is your teacher. Embrace it, and learn from it!

AUDIENCE SAFETY

The more authentic and genuine you are, the more people feel safe and open up.

Safety is the most important ingredient for building a presentation of impact. If an audience feels unsafe, uncertain, or even defensive, they will cancel you out. Audiences need to know:

- What is happening?
- Where are they going?
- What is expected from them?

People need to feel invited to express their ideas and be free from attack and negative consequences. No matter how assertive and experienced an audience appears, there is always a territory of caution:

- Who's observing this?
- What reports will be sent to the boss?
- If I speak up, will I sound uninformed?
- Maybe this is a stupid question?
- I don't want to risk looking dumb!

Though everyone's perception of safety differs, there are some guidelines that hold true with most audiences. Speakers communicate safety through (1) structure, (2) use of the familiar, (3) answers, solutions, and techniques, (4) helping the audience feel right, and (5) building trust.

1. STRUCTURE IS SAFE

Audiences feel safe with some structure. High structure people are safe with order, formality, and clear boundaries. Low structure people feel safe with open spaces, informality, and improvisation. The speaker has to know and respect the structural needs of an audience. How you structure and organize your talk communicates at a safety level. There are five areas where you can define and adjust to their structural needs:

With High-Structure Audiences	**With Low-Structure Audiences**
1. How you Organize Your Talk	
These audiences want to know where you are at all points in your talk. They want a logical, linear progression of points. If they get lost, they will think *you* are not organized. Inform them ahead what to expect and what they will learn. Later tell them what they have learned.	These audiences don't require a road map of exactly where they are at all times. Your structure can be less linear and more fluid. Explore with them what they have learned.
2. How You Attend to Time Lines	
Keep strict time commitments; begin and end on time. If you have to start late, keep the audience updated. Ending times are inviolate. Keep breaks and process groups strictly to the allotted times. Refer often to time lines.	Keep time commitments as best you can, but you don't have to be a slave to the clock. If you stretch out a break or group process, it's usually OK as long as everyone is involved. You don't have to keep referring to time lines, but all audiences appreciate your respect for *their* time.
3. How You Handle Formalities	
Formal introductions and acknowledgments are comfortable. Business or formal attire is usually expected.	Informality and spontaneity are comfortable. Surprises, deviating from the expected order, and informal dress are all accepted within good taste.

With High-Structure Audiences	With Low-Structure Audiences

4. How You Use Details

Specific answers and techniques, ways to practice, books to read, and classes to take—all create the feeling of safety. Give enough detail for them to work on their own. Tell them specifically what to do and what results to expect.

Tips and techniques, ways to practice, books to read, and classes to take are always welcome, but these groups want to be pointed in the right direction, and given open-ended suggestions and benchmark results to look for.

5. How You Use Handouts

The handout should have clear, linear format, contain specific detail, and be something they can follow step-by-step. Stay with the handout! If you jump around, you'll confuse them.

The handout should give necessary information and serve as a resource after your speech. You're not constrained to follow it exactly, though the more linear and detailed the format, the more you probably need to stay with it.

2. The Familiar Is Safe

Audiences feel safe with what is familiar.

They like to hear their own names, their own language and expressions, and their own ways of thinking. Because they make the unconscious assumption that the familiar is safe territory, it's important that the speaker know the language and issues of the audience. The process of building rapport is the process of extending what is familiar.

Ways to Build the Familiar

1. Open with a surprise story that involves the audience.
2. Incorporate in your opening remarks a phrase that you've heard them use.

3. Mention people in the audience by name.
4. Refer to something you have recently shared with the audience.
5. Call attention to an event, a common interest or goal that links you.
6. Use *their* vocabulary whenever possible.
7. Directly meet any issue that is on everyone's mind.
8. Give voice to what they are saying in their heads.
9. Meet their expectations.

Take small steps into the unfamiliar, but always return to that safe territory where audiences trust and relax. Safety resides in the known.

3. Answers, Solutions, and Techniques Are Safe

People love those five easy techniques because they sound like a safe, quick fix. A spoonful of sweet answers can help the bitter truth go down, but when there are no sweet answers, speakers are challenged to satisfy the audience's appetite while keeping intact their own integrity to speak the truth. A closer look at answers, solutions, and techniques may tell us how to do this.

An Answer Is a *Response*

The audience complains, "They don't respond to us! Give us an answer!" The speaker replies with:

1. *Information:* expert knowledge and informed opinion.
2. *Expanded vision:* big picture, connections, possibilities, and cautions.
3. *Directness:* feedback and discussion.

Answers come in the form of: (1) a confirmation, confirming what they have been thinking all along; (2) a new idea, building a connection with the new information; or (3) the "Aaaa," suddenly things fit—maybe *this* is the answer!

An Answer Is Individualized Knowing

The principal job of the speaker is to help audiences identify their own answers, not to present a bag of dazzling absolutes that leave them where they started. Easy answers are hard work! That's why audiences want the speaker to come up with them. The speaker clears the way, reveals the basic structure, helps people prioritize and utilize information. The speaker does the prework and presents a kind of do-it-yourself kit that is three-hole-punched with easy-to-read instructions.

In music, the *answer* of a fugue is the imitation or exact transposition of a theme by a different voice. As speakers, we often give form to the answers already in the minds of the audience by presenting to them a different voice.

A Solution Is an *Action*

A *solution* is an answer in action, the process for solving a problem, changing the dynamics, lessening the negative impact, clearing up confusion, and making the situation better.

The solution is how you solve the problem.

A Technique Is a Way of *Implementing* the Solution

Techniques involve skill levels, style, approach, and procedure. Note how *answer, solution,* and *technique* support each other:

Answer: *What*	Solution: *How*	Technique: *Way*
Example 1: The answer is to reduce costs.	The solution is to devise and implement a reduction plan.	The first technique is to prioritize expenses.
Example 2: The answer is to change myself.	The solution is to check my feelings.	The first technique is to practice journal writing.
Example 3: The answer is to build a team.	The solution is to devise a plan of implementation.	The first technique is to rotate the leadership role.

Speakers are hired to bring answers, solutions, and techniques. Brochures present an impressive list of what the audience will receive. I've always believed that if people get one practical idea or process that they can implement, they have their money's worth. You can be the voice that provides a response, a process, a way to accomplish. Your guarantees are authenticity, expertise, cutting-edge knowledge, and customization to audience needs.

4. Being Right Is Safe!

Nobody wants to be wrong. Everyone deserves a little face saving. Part of preparing a safe atmosphere for an audience is to provide a place where no one is made wrong. This means the speaker always:

- ■ Makes people right: there are no bad guys in the audience or in the larger organization.
- ■ Acknowledges the positive part of any audience contribution.
- ■ Goes to the aid of anyone "made wrong" by another person in the group.

This skill of "making right" rests on the speaker's own tolerance to be made wrong. In order for a speaker to create a safe environment, where no one in the audience is made wrong, that speaker has to give up the *necessity* of being right him- or herself. Audiences will point out your flaws, barb their questions, tell you that you didn't when you did, and give you a label based on a faulty assumption. If you bite into the worm of self-defense, you not only move into an unsafe place for yourself but, by the very act of self-justification, you make the other person wrong. I'm not suggesting that the speaker submit to abuse and false accusations; that in itself would create a really unsafe atmosphere for everyone. I am saying that the speaker's job is to be audience focused and stay completely away from personal defensiveness. Here are some "nevers" for every speaker:

1. *Never use the words, "You are wrong."* A person or group may voice a faulty assumption, be a minority of one, speak out of line, and even make you wrong. Even though you have opposite views, no one makes anyone wrong! You recognize it's their own need to be right that is showing. Watch your voice tone; judgment doesn't need words. Don't take them down; handle it in a way that allows everyone to save face.

2. *Never set someone up to be wrong.* I've seen speakers try to "get in" with the audience by allowing the bosses, management, or the company to be cast as the "bad guy." Role playing can sometimes be a setup for embarrassment as a willing participant can look foolish or fall into a mistake that is commonly made. Sometimes whole audiences are set up for failure by well-meaning organizations that stack the attendance with people who are not safe together: workers who do not feel safe speaking up when their bosses are present, first-level military who are expected to openly contribute in the presence of uniformed officers, kids with their parents. I remem-

ber a group of high-level "observers" who filed across the back of a room and sat down while I struggled to encourage spontaneous participation from a stunned and immediately silenced group.

3. *Never leave an open wound.* Be sensitive to anyone who might be hurting or feeling wrong as a result of group pressure or incomplete handling of a situation. Take time to acknowledge, to thank, and to say how everyone's contribution helps the learning process. Sometimes people can come off as being really funny when they make a mistake. Don't be fooled by their ability to laugh it off; thank them for the learning. Make them right!

4. *Never speak ill about anyone on or off the platform.* Be careful not to make fun of anyone or use their name in an unflattering light. Even off the platform, it's amazing how quickly a careless word, thoughtlessly spoken, can reach unintended ears. I almost lost a contract once because of a side remark I made to another passenger in a Chicago airport cab. I didn't even hear my remark; yet within hours, it was being repeated by the top management, just a flip of the tongue, not meant to offend anyone. Be very careful!

5. Trusting the Speaker Is Safe

Any perceived personal agenda on the part of a speaker can label that speaker unsafe:

- She's just in it for the glory.
- He's in management's pocket.
- She's not really interested in us.

Building trust can be a tough call for the speaker who is hired to motivate people to buy into an unpopular decision or a change that has already been determined. Smoke out any hidden agenda that puts you in the middle. The speaker must be able to honestly communicate to an audience from the ground of his or her own integrity. Speakers are perceived trustworthy who are congruent (words, actions, attitudes, physical appearance, props—all must communicate *one* message), open and frank, who speak their language, who hear and respond to the audience.

No Bugs

I remember being in the Smithsonian Institute in Washington, D. C, when an advance team from the White House suddenly descended on us to prepare for a Presidential visit. In came the starched men with walkie-talkies and the dogs sniffing for possible explosive devices to thoroughly debug the building before the President arrived. We don't bring walkie-talkies or dogs, but as speakers we do look for possible glitches and potential explosives that can threaten our safe space. Here are some ways we do this.

1. *Check the personnel.* Who is going to be there; what's the representation and diversity? Is anyone likely to come with a loaded handgun in his or her pocket (speaking figuratively, of course); are there any recent battles or skirmishes that you should know about? Check out any potential problems that might create an "unsafe" atmosphere.

A poignant example of an audience feeling unsafe happened to me in Hong Kong. I was presenting a seminar on "Assertive Management" with the "big boss" sitting in the audience, carefully watching everyone. He used the break times to openly poll people on exactly what they were getting from the material. Everyone felt unsafe; it was wrecking-ball time, and the impact wasn't the one I was going for.

2. *Find any time bombs and defuse them.* Check for hidden agendas and unrealistic expectations. Get clear about what you can and cannot affect, and clarify a realistic expectation of what you can deliver. Know why you're there, and sniff out any surrounding events that could impede your effectiveness.

We ask an audience to listen to us, to trust our credibility, and put themselves in our hands. Egos are fragile; self-esteem is often a veneer. The speaker/trainer is responsible for "securing the area" and keeping it secure so that all know it is safe to walk here.

IMPACT BREAKS THROUGH SAFETY WALLS

The poet Robert Frost wrote that good fences make good neighbors. Never try to tear down an audience's defenses; they put them up for a reason. Even though some defenses get solidified into soundproof walls of fear with behaviors that can block success, each person has the right to his or her own protections. When people feel safe, they stop defending their walls. Impact happens when a chunk falls off the wall, when some sound or light gets through, or when the wall just disappears. Content, answers, and techniques do not bring down walls; they just keep us feeling safe.

THE SPEAKER DEFINES THE SPACE

"You're in my face!"

"Stand back so I can get a good look at you!"

"He keeps me at arm's length!"

"Did you notice, she never gets close?"

Space communicates!

"Deceptively classical on the outside, forthrightly modern and light on the inside" was the *New York Times*'s description of architect James Freed's design of the new San Francisco Public Library. It was hailed as a light-filled space with room for the imagination. What a great description for the speaker, because, with every presentation, we adjust our space to fit both the speaker and the audience. As environmental architects, we are always working with three variables: sight, sound, and feel.

SIGHT

Space perception is not only a matter of what can be perceived but what can be screened out.

E. T. Hall, *The Hidden Dimension*

Check the Look of the Room

When you walk into the meeting room, is the look of that room congruent with your talk? Consider the challenge if you're talk is on "Saving the Environment" and the auditorium displays a stuffed moose head hanging center stage. Or if your speech is on "Organizing Clutter," and extra tables and chairs are cluttering the back of the room. Are you lost in a ballroom trying to talk on intimacy or attempting to lead a team-building session in an airplane hanger?

Consider each space with an eye to bringing it, as much as possible, visually in line with your presentation. If the moose head cannot come down, it can be used as a visual demonstration of the fate of endangered animals. Clutter can be cleared, and if you're eclipsed in a ballroom, build an intimate space by pulling a pioneer survival strategy: "Circle the wagons" and bring everyone in close.

Check the Lighting

Restaurants are notorious for dim, romantic lighting that may dissuade a closer examination of the meal but can make it tough to bring a subject to light. Can everyone see your face? If you use notes, can you read them? Be adamant about light; it's never perfect, but there must be enough and in the right places.

Check the Audience's Line of Vision

Where does the eye look? James Freed designed the San Francisco Library with glass walls and doors to invite the eye to roam. You, however, want the roaming eyes of the audience to focus on you, so be careful where you position yourself in relationship to glass partitions or walls of windows.

1. *Obstructions:* Are there visual obstructions, like support pillars? Can everyone view an undistorted screen? "Spot sit" around the room, and check it out.

2. *Distractions:* Take out the leftover material on boards and flip charts from a previous speaker. If there's a coffee and tea setup, make sure it's in the back of the room or out of the line of sight. Check the placement of the clock, and if possible, set up the room to discourage continual clock watching.

3. *Room Setup:* The visual flow of the room setup should direct eyes to the speaker. I have found two room setups to be particularly helpful in bringing people together and directing the sight line. The first is the "sunburst" setup, because it places the speaker center front and angles the tables and chairs out from that center like a sunburst forming a large semicircle around the speaker. Tables are placed end-to-end, forming a long row and angled toward the speaker; chairs face forward on each side. I've used this setup to great advantage with large audiences; it has the space-saving quality of theater style with the added advantage of a table from which to work. The sunburst setup is friendly, allows people to see each other, and softens the linear formation format.

The second setup is similar but used when the interactive process calls for table groups of four to six people. Again, start center front with the speaker and position the tables away from the speaker in a modified semicircle. Both of these room setups maximize the space, provide a friendly atmosphere where people can see and hear each other, and draw the line of sight to the speaker.

SOUND

When reduction of auditory interference made it possible to conduct the meeting without undue strain, complaints about the chairman ceased.

E. T. Hall, *The Hidden Dimension*

Speaking on team building in an airplane hangar was a real challenge. It was actually a dirigible hangar where the airplanes looked like toys sitting on the floor of a large open mouth! We were directed to an area away from traffic but surrounded by a constant roar that magnified through this giant echo chamber, and we could not escape the sound assault.

Most acoustical difficulties are not that extreme, but there is often the clank of dishes coming from the restaurant kitchen, the recorded music over the hotel intercom, street noises from the open windows, and interference from the group on the other side of the room partition. If you've done much speaking in hotels, you know that the partitions that divide meeting rooms are hardly soundproof. If you can find out ahead of time when your sound levels might conflict, you may do some preadjusting. If they're "just showing a film," remember that the sound track will amplify through a partition louder than a live voice.

FEEL

Cutting down on movement in the peripheral field will reduce the sense of crowding.

E. T. Hall, *The Hidden Dimension*

How does the space feel? If it feels sterile and cold, perhaps you can warm it up with some taped music before the meeting begins, a bright banner, or colorful handouts. Will there be enough air supply? Hotel ventilation, at best, is usually inadequate, and a crowded room calls for air supplementation. If it's a contest between noise from the open windows and fresh air, opt for the air. The room must feel inviting, comfortable, and efficient.

TOUGH LESSONS IN SPACE

The issue is not control but dynamic connectedness.

Sally Helgesen, *The Web of Inclusion*

Every speaker can pull up a list of horror stories about tough spaces they have worked. Here are a few of mine, along with the lessons I learned.

Lesson #1: Check Out the Room Ahead of Time!

I once conducted a training session in the basement room where the Allies broke the Japanese code during the Second World War. It was a cramped, underground space called the "code room," buried underneath one of the main buildings at Pearl Harbor. Throughout the war, code breakers worked around the clock in this remote place that no one knew existed—no windows, one door, very quiet. And this was our training space! On Monday morning, 45 participants filed down the stairs into the obscurity of the airless, subterranean room where we would practice team building for five days. This was no executive survival course: Interaction down there was like gymnastics in a submarine. It really turned us into a team with fresh-air breaks every half hour and physical exercises on the commander's lawn.

Lesson #2: Check Out the Action on the Other Side of the Partition!

I remember trying to compete with a retirement breakfast on the other side of our hotel meeting room partition. I was speaking on "How to Handle People with Tact and Skill," when a New Orleans jazz band started up with "When the

Saints Go Marching In," and what sounded like a roomful of people kicking back their chairs and marching around the room. We quickly opted for an early coffee break, while I attempted to regroup. Given our options, we decided to go with it and consider it an extra benefit not listed in the promotional brochure.

Lesson #3: Be Prepared to Improvise!

I spoke one time to a group of over 100 people at a Michigan Avenue hotel on Chicago's north shore. The room was approximately 15 feet wide and 80 feet long. With no other rooms available, I ordered risers to elevate myself, took away all tables, and used the hallways for breakout sessions. I fought the discomfort of the setup all day; it was like speaking to a long queue.

Lesson #4: Utilize Everything!

Then there was a five-day seminar in Eureka, California, where the only available meeting space for the 30 participants was a ground-level motel suite wedged between the divided lanes of the freeway as it went through town. It was February, the rainy season, and logging trucks steamed by our windows, throwing water up onto the building with such jarring force that we had to wait midsentence for them to pass. The audience was a group of young forest service supervisors who were used to challenges and loved sitting on the floor, rocking with the logging trucks, and participating in a spontaneous training session. The whole scene became a metaphor of what the supervisors face every day: tough conditions, inadequate resources, and constant change. This week was "real," and we used everything to our advantage.

Lesson #5: Impact Can Happen in the Darndest Places!

We were in the tropics; the heat was terrible. The swamp fans made so much noise that my voice was giving out, and I couldn't hear myself. The men had taken off their shirts, soaked them in water, and draped them over their heads while the women looked on jealously as they suffered in silence. Calling a break, we all gathered up buckets, dishes, and pails from the kitchen, filled them with water and put our feet in them. It was my first and only speech delivered while standing barefoot in a pail of water, but it did the job. It turned out to be a powerful session even though we looked like a scene from the operating room of the TV show, "Mash."

Conditions are never perfect; you learn to deal with what you have. You get what you can, you improvise with what you can find, and utilize everything. The space has to be right for both the speaker and the audience.

SPEAKER SPACE

The space needs of every speaker are different; know and respect yours.

As they say during takeoff, first secure your own air mask—then help others! Take care of yourself, meet your own space needs first: (1) breathing space, (2) working space, (3) perceptual space, and (4) impact space. Here's how it works.

1. Give Yourself Breathing Space

"Push" energy moves you forward, but the pause gives everything a chance to breathe.

Your breath is the foundation of your physical and emotional power; therefore, learn to take short and unobserved breathing breaks. Here's how to do it:

1. Center yourself.

■ Get grounded! Feel the whole surface of both feet firmly on the floor. If you're sitting, touch the outer surface of each foot on the floor so that the edge of each foot connects solidly with the ground.

■ Relax your mind; stop any self-talk that's going on in your head.

■ Center your focus, be entirely present in the moment. Move your focus to the audience and what you've come here to do.

2. Take a slow, deep breath.

■ Take the breath from as far down in your body as you can; pull it up from your genitals.

■ Hold it for a few seconds.

3. Release the breath.

■ As you release your breath, let go of any tension or stress.

■ Consciously relax your muscles and any tightness you feel.

■ Release completely. Take it down to where there is no breath left and hold it there for a few seconds. Empty out your lungs, and hold that empty state as long as you can without straining.

■ Release the pressure of doing a good job, of not forgeting your talk, of reaching your goal, and just be *quiet* in the moment.

■ Repeat the process.

When to Create Breathing Space

Creating breathing space any time you recognize being at one of the following places:

■ Just before you begin your talk.

■ When you are feeling nervous.

■ At transition time, within your talk.

■ If you go blank or lose your place.

■ When the audience throws you an unexpected challenge.

■ When you realize you're racing the clock to get it all in.

■ When you notice that you're pushing hard and your body has tensed.

■ When you're not having fun.

Believe it or not, these are the times when you often stop breathing and survive on shallow air intake. High-energy speaking on thin air is a real pull on your energy and leaves your nervous system unstable as well as exhausted. It only takes a second to breathe. Practice using this technique to restore your breathing space

2. Make Sure You Have Enough Working Space

What you can do in a space determines how you experience it.

The speaker needs:

1. Room for movement.
2. A place for all materials and props.
3. Some separation from the audience.

Speaker–Audience Separation

As some grab front-row seats at the movie theater, and others climb to the last row of the balcony, so it is with the space needs of speakers and audiences. Some speakers like that front-row connection; they want to be physically close. Other speakers need some physical distance to keep the clarity of their focus. Both preferences seek a working space that supports audience rapport.

Edward T. Hall, in his ground-breaking classic *The Hidden Dimension,* identified four separations of space between people that every speaker should consider when designing room setups and working space: (1) intimate distance, (2) personal distance, (3) social distance, and (4) public distance. Based on Hall's calculations, here are some adaptations for the speaker:

1. *Intimate distance: 18–20 inches.* We are generally uncomfortable when this boundary is transgressed, as in a crowded elevator or on a bus. At this distance, details are enlarged, and vision is often blurred, resulting in sight and sound distortion.

   Adaptation for the Speaker: Some speaking spaces pack you in, and, if you have to use one, make sure the front-row people feel reasonably comfortable. If there is almost no space between you, try to work away from them when possible. Reduce height distortion by sitting down; soften your voice and reduce gesturing.

2. *Personal distance: 18–40 inches.* This is just beyond the range of touch and feels safe to most people. Your hand gestures are easily seen, and your voice comes through clearly. Most body heat or nervousness is not perceptible at this distance.

   Adaptation for the Speaker: Topics of personal involvement are compatible with this distance. Since front-row tables and seats are usually within this range, people who choose them signify that they both are interested and want to be closely involved in the process.

3. *Social distance: 4–7 feet.* The whole speaker is easily seen surrounded by additional space. Most small- to medium-size audiences fall within this speaker–audience distance.

   Adaptation for the Speaker: This space is for discussing impersonal topics with some involvement. Groups who are particularly cautious can feel comfortable here, as the speaker moves from impersonal to more personal subjects. Audiences can also screen out the speaker at this distance without appearing rude.

4. *Public Distance: 12–25 feet.* Facial details are no longer visible to an audience. The speaker starts to take on a flatter look, less three-dimensional; the speaker's head gets smaller.

   Adaptation for the Speaker: A microphone is probably needed. Enlarged video can provide the attention to detail that is lost in this space.

5. *Public Distance: 25 feet +.* The nonverbal part of communication shifts to gestures and body stance. The speaker is seen as small and within a setting.

   Adaptation for the Speaker: Everything must be exaggerated or amplified by audio/video and/or gestures.

Bridging the Gap

There is always some physical distance between you and the audience; the question is, how much do you want? Intimate and more personal topics call for shorter distances; social and public topics allow larger distances. Audio and video are used to complement and correct distance imbalances.

Not all distance is physical! An even more powerful gap is the distance that is perceived and felt. New situations and first time interactions, preconceived expectations, and critical judgments can separate speaker from audience, causing a gap that has to be bridged before any impact can happen. One of the keys to reducing this perceptual distance I call "the skill of intimacy."

3. Know Your Perceptual Space

True distance is not the concern of the eye; it is granted only to the spirit.

Antoine de Saint-Exupéry, *Flight to Arras*

An intimate style extends far beyond the warm fuzzies of motivational speaking. It's that quality in your speaking that draws people, that evaporates separation and blends you and the audience into one. It adapts to and strengthens every situation where connection needs to be made. The intimate speaker has three unique qualities: (1) the ability to establish quickly, (2) the capacity to know and communicate from the inside, and (3) the presence to communicate appreciation and interest to an audience.

1. *The ability to establish quickly.* In James Clavel's novel *Shogun* it was said of the main character, Toranaga, that he could walk up and down before his troops, and, as he silently passed them, each man felt personally addressed. Instant connection! We meet and immediately feel comfortable with each other, connected. The speaker reduces perceptual space with this skill of personal connection.

2. *The capacity to know and communicate from the inside.* You've walked in their shoes and know their road. Intimate knowledge implies information and understanding from either a long association, a similar experience, or a thorough study and observation. The more the audience perceives you to have this intimate knowledge of them and their situation, the more you reduce any space between you.

3. *The presence to communicate appreciation and interest.* A warm, personal attitude of caring and acknowledgment brings people together; intimacy involves seeing each other. In business and on the platform, when the speaker naturally and honestly extends this quality, a sense of mutuality can happen. We hear comments from our audiences like:

- "She was so warm and friendly; it was as if I knew her."
- "Would you believe, he remembered my name?"
- "I felt like he was talking just to me."
- "He was never a stranger with us, always one of us."
- "She let us see something of herself, something of who she is."

We associate this quality of intimacy with private conversations, candlelit dinners, familiar groups, and cozy spaces. But even in large auditoriums and big conference rooms, the perception of intimacy can be felt. In formal, stiff, and grand spaces speaker and audience can share the qualities of warmth, appreciation, knowledge, and openness. The skill of intimacy is the ability to draw people to you and relax them in your presence. As a speaker, no matter what your content, a style that is unadorned, honest, and personal will bridge and reduce the perceptual distance between you and an audience.

4. Leave Room for Impact Space!

When the heart opens, it will rain.

Sometimes we're moving so fast that we forget to collect what we came for. We know that audiences have a built-in antenna for closing time so we speak faster and hit the goal line without factoring in time for everyone to pick up their trophies. We race the clock and often fail to leave two or three minutes at the end for people to assimilate and take in the impact. Here are some thoughts for ensuring that space.

Promise Only What You Can Deliver Comfortably

Too many marketing promises can lash you to an impossible and frayed outcome as you desperately try to cram everything in and never quite make it. With pressure on the speaker for high content, it takes clarity, honesty with yourself, and a degree of courage to realistically define what you can and cannot deliver. To promise too much produces a huge amount of stress. Don't buy into it!

Back-Time Your Speech

When I was a radio director, in order to get a finished show off the air within a 15-second time cushion, I learned the skill of back timing. It goes like this:

1. Start with the parameter of your beginning and ending times. Example:

Begin	9:00 A.M.
Close	9:30 A.M.
Total speaking time	30 minutes

2. Figure out approximately how much time each section will take. Example:

Begin	9:00 A.M.
Introduction	2 minutes
Main point	3 minutes
Action step	5 minutes
Questions/answers	5 minutes
Conclusion	3 minutes
Close	9:30 A.M.
Total speaking time	18 minutes
Cushion time for improvising	12 minutes

3. Now, check the cushion.

   A late start? You speak slower than anticipated? More questions from the audience than expected? The audience opens up an area of your topic that takes more time? How much spontaneity do you want? You may not need a 12-minute cushion. It's all a matter of knowing your own style and being in touch with your time and space needs.

4. Preselect areas that can be shortened or expanded. Ask yourself:

   a. Where can I cut?

   b. Where and how can I lengthen?

   c. At what specific places do I need to be on target?

5. Identify your check points.

Begin introduction	9:00 A.M.
Begin action step	9:15 A.M.
Begin conclusion	9:25 A.M.
Close	9:30 A.M.

Now before you say, "Wait a minute, how can I be going for impact when I'm counting seconds?" Relax! Note what you have done:

1. You have prepared, refined, and practiced your most efficient time frame.
2. You have identified the places you need to be on track!
3. You have built in an advance warning system for yourself.
4. You have allowed discretionary time for spontaneity, audience response, and slower pace.
5. You have ensured enough time for a strong close.

I carry a tiny clock with a large face and place it strategically where I can get a quick look without anyone noticing. Back timing will reduce your stress level, and your talk will come out wonderfully spontaneous and sounding almost extemporaneous when it is actually timed to the second.

AUDIENCE SPACE

A common space provides a common ground and common ground is essential to flourish.

Sally Helgesen, *The Web of Inclusion*

Territory is established so rapidly that even the second session in a series of lectures is sufficient to find a significant proportion of most audiences back in the same seats.

E. T. Hall, *The Hidden Dimension*

When a person walks into a meeting room and looks over the available seats, the place that person chooses to sit is the seat where he or she feels the most comfortable. Some grab those back-row seats near the door, while others go to the ends of rows or back up against a wall. Sensitivity to the audience's space needs involves awareness and protection of their (1) breathing space, (2) seeing and hearing space, (3) moving space, and (4) reflective and decision space.

1. Protect *Their* Breathing Space

The TV commercial featuring the little old lady in a jammed subway car who smiles up at the man towering above her as she tells him, "I've enjoyed your breath since 96th Street," is a pleasant laugh, but my guess is that most of us prefer not to breathe the garlic sandwich he ate for lunch. Some physical distance and oxygen-fresh air is essential, and you, the speaker, must monitor the oxygen level in the room. The smaller the room, the less oxygen; if there is no way to keep that oxygen replenished, give the group more breaks. You can even go so far as to ask people to go outside during a break and tank up on oxygen. Audiences can surprise you at how well they handle other space infringements, but they must have oxygen to function.

2. Ensure *Their* Seeing and Hearing Space

Everyone needs to be able to see everything! Sit in the audience yourself, try several places in the room, and check out what you can or cannot see. Everyone should hear everything, both speaker and audience comments. Make sure that people speak up when they give comments from the audience; repeat often.

3. Create Moving Space

My immediate question when I first walk into the meeting or banquet room is: "Can we all move around in this space, physically and emotionally?" I then begin to figure out my adjustments.

Interactive Spaces

Interaction means movement and connection. I often say to an audience that I want everyone to: (1) meet as many people as possible, (2) make at least one new business contact or friend, and (3) enjoy the experience. For this to happen, I have to know something about placing and moving people. Here are some tips:

- *If you want two people to talk with each other,* sit them at the corner of a table at a right angle to each other. It has been researched that cross-corner conversations are more frequent than any other position at a table.

- *If you want to create the sense of a more expansive space,* cut down on any movement in the peripheral parts of the room. This reduces any sense of crowding and maximizes the actual working space.

- *Don't move people too quickly.* Let people fully establish themselves in a space before moving them. If you're using table groups, let people get fully acquainted with each other before you switch them to other people. If the audience is seated in rows, encourage each to have contact with the people closest to them. After initial connections are made, you can even move them around the room with short-term activities, but let them return to their originally chosen seat.

- *Get comfortable with people's reactions.* I've noticed that nonmovers fall into three behaviors around space change: First, there are the people who refuse to move. They stake out their territory, and if anyone else takes the seat, they let them know it's theirs. Then, there is the guy who grabs the seat in the corner with his back up against the wall and, when everyone switches places, you find him in his original seat. Finally, there are the folks who move but not very far. They stay at the same table with only a slight shift. That way, they get a new group without having to make a major change. Fortunately, most are able to take their "home base" with them and can move around freely.

▪ *Lunch break is a good time to make a major space change* in full-day sessions. Give moving instructions before the break.

▪ *Don't force a change!* If I sense the group is really hesitant or doesn't want to move, I explain the benefits and let the group make the decision.

Breakout Spaces

▪ Breakout spaces can be used to great advantage as they give people a chance to move around. They can extend the actual space of the meeting room, provide a change of scene, and give opportunity for everyone to participate. Almost any space can be used for breakout: hotel hallways, small sitting areas, coffee shops, outdoor benches, and lawns. Once we even used the ladies' restroom to serve as a simulated office for low-level employees. This location actually gave strength to their negotiation for more prestigious office quarters, and we had fun with the metaphors that came with that location! It carried its own impact!

Meeting Room Space

Maximize participant space. Don't clog up the room with large tables. I remember a huge conference table that took up an entire room where I was supposed to stand at one end, and the small audience was to squeeze into the remaining space. I asked for it to be removed and replaced with narrow single tables or to have a room change.

Clear unnecessary furniture. Remove extra tables, unnecessary chalk boards, and anything else that you will not be using. Sometimes you have to be quite insistent and promise to put everything back. Whatever it takes, set up your own space to fit your needs.

Remember: Reserve the space for people, not furniture. Use all *your space. Expanding minds and spirits need expanded space.*

4. Provide Reflective and Decision Space

People Need Room for an Idea to Sink In

They need to hear it, see it, touch it, and talk about it. Be careful not to rush past an "Aaa." Don't be afraid of the pause, the empty space.

People Want Context

They want to see the connections to the bigger picture, connections to themselves, to each other, and to their own experiences.

People Need Time to Process an Idea

They need to follow the logical sequences, identify specifics, make application, and decide on an action step. None of this can be rushed. If you try to cover too much, you leave the audience exhausted, confused, and feeling inadequate because they didn't quite get it. If too much is thrown at them too quickly, they have no space to assimilate and choose what they need.

10 THE SPEAKER LIGHTS THE ENERGY

In front of an audience
Do you ever feel
Isolated?
Adhering to some image of
What you think is expected,
Frequently
Emotionally drained?

*The energy we radiate is crucial in determining
what we attract to ourselves!*

Susan Butcher, veteran winner in the Alaskan Iditarod
dogsled races, is known for winning races without wearing
down her team. Every day of the race her team gets stronger,
and they finish at full power! There is a metaphor here for us.
We do the right things for a winning presentation: We
research, customize, structure, and practice as though this is
it, this is our only reality! Yet, impact happens on an *energy*
level. In the final take, our ability to finish at full power is a
matter of how we utilize our energy.

OUR VOICES ARE ENERGY

We're sitting in a crowded restaurant, enjoying an intimate
conversation when suddenly, penetrating voices intrude. The

man at the next table is caught up in telling a story, and the woman in the corner has had too much to drink. No matter how much we try to tune them out, their voices cut in and change the energy of our conversation.

- Some voices are dissonant, harsh, shrill, and precise, like their owners.
- Some voices boom and crash, some tinkle and laugh.
- Some voices put you to sleep with their sameness and lack of cadence.
- Some are weak, whimpering, and apologetic.
- There are intruding voices and begging voices.
- There are seductive voices and dismissal voices.
- There are alive voices and corpse voices.
- There are healing voices!

Voices project the source and the quality of our energy. If we're relaxed, our voice says it. When we feel tension, stress or weariness, it tells in our voice. When the telephone jars us out of a deep sleep, no matter how much we try to sound like we've been up for hours, inevitably comes the response, "Oh, did I wake you up?" Our voice tells it all!

To give voice to a thought is to give energy and power to the thought. Speaking is serious business, because voice is sound, and sound is resonance. And resonance amplifies who we are, why we're here, and what comes across to others. We may fool ourselves, but our voices tell the truth to an audience.

OUR THOUGHTS ARE ENERGY

What are you really *thinking* as you wait to begin your speech?

- "This looks like a tough group to crack!"
- "Why are there so many empty seats?"
- "If I can just get through this without forgetting!"

- ▪ "What's my opening line?"
- ▪ "Oh, my God, the place is packed!"

When we most need power, fear tries to sabotage us. We're artists at finding our own jugular; just thinking a fearful thought gives it power. It's imperative to run a tight edit on the script of our self-talk before we face an audience.

Athletes learn to discipline their minds in order to take their performances to a new level. Speaking calls for this same mental discipline; otherwise, our thoughts will move in random patterns, usually stopping on something painful or disturbing. Unless you know how to give order to your thoughts, attention will go to whatever is most problematic at the moment, and if you're waiting to walk before an audience, there's little doubt about the moment.

Develop habits that can control this random sabotage. Delete any negative thought such as, *"If I can just get through the first point without crashing . . . "* Think only about what you want to happen, not what you want to avoid. Put down the hand mirror that magnifies your distortions, and censor all those imperatives such as *having* to make a good impression, *having* to win them over, and, especially, *having to make an impact.* Position your thoughts to reinforce only the results that you want.

The Results You *Want*

- ▪ Do you want people to think seriously about a specific issue?
- ▪ Do you want to move people to an action?
- ▪ Do you want to touch their emotions?

If you don't know exactly what you want, you won't generate the energy for it. The clearer and more in detail you can see what you want, the more energy you release to make it happen.

The Results You *Expect*

There's a big step between *wanting* something and *expecting* it. It's our expectations that summon our results; what we really expect is what we get! Take the risk of expecting something that you do not yet see, and have the courage to accept it when it comes. "Fine-tune" your self-talk so that every thought gives power to that expectation.

> Get in touch with your real intention.
> Move past survival,
> Past giving the perfect speech,
> Past impressing.
> Get out of your head
> And get to what your heart understands!
> It's all there—but you have to do it!

IMPACT IS ENERGY

One afternoon in San Francisco, I was on my way to something important when I heard a solitary voice, exquisite, as I had never heard before. One undulating line of pure soprano drew me to the 64-foot-high dome of an outdoor rotunda, where a woman was standing alone holding a metal bowl and singing. There were no words, just beautiful soprano tones that filled the space as she accompanied herself by rubbing the rim of the Tibetan singing bowl in her hands. As though time had stopped, people had frozen midstep; it was such a compelling sound that everyone under the dome stood zapped within its impact.

On an energy level, we create the forms that draw people to us! It is impossible to remain dead in the presence of something or someone totally alive. As speakers, so much of our focus is on producing a speech that will sell—one we can package and promote. The real impact we seek comes not from the package but from the moment. The woman under the dome had carefully thought through her presentation, but it was only in the actual moment of her improvisation that her presentation turned into impact. Each speech has to have the energy of "brand new." There is no automatic pilot; we cannot create, practice, and make a hundred copies, because there's no impact in the copy.

It's in the moment of birth that the cry of life comes!

How do we give birth to speech after speech, keeping each speech fresh and ourselves alive? How do we build and maintain this impact of energy?

FIRST: TAME THE AUDIENCE

"I cannot play with you," said the fox, "I am not tamed."
"What does that mean, tame?" asked the little prince.
"It means to establish ties."

Antoine de Saint-Exupéry, *The Little Prince*

Some audiences are tough to tame; we barely get to know them. We give our speech and move on to the next; some days, audiences even start to look alike. In *The Little Prince*, the fox was like a hundred thousand other foxes and the boy like a hundred thousand other little boys—until they *cared* enough to connect. Albert Einstein could have been speaking directly to speakers when he said:

> Our task is to free ourselves from this prison of discon-
> nection, by widening our circle of compassion to
> embrace all living creatures and the whole of nature in
> its beauty.

We're so used to thinking of compassion as an emotion of concern for the less fortunate that we miss the real power of its energy. "It's the key to how we connect with people; it means "with passion." We may dazzle and entertain an audience, but we won't tame them unless we really care.

It was the American folk hero, Will Rogers, the first mayor of Beverly Hills, California, and a consummate entertainer to world audiences, who was quoted as saying that he never met a man he didn't like. I wonder if we can say that about audiences? We have to like the audience; what we're feeling about them as we begin a speech can spell the difference between an OK speech and one with impact. Compassion is the key that allows us to be tamed and to see the audience as uniquely special.

> *If you tame me, it will be as if the sun came to shine on my life. I make you my friend and now you are unique in all the world.*
>
> Antoine de Saint-Exupéry, *The Little Prince*

SECOND: BUILD THE ENERGY CIRCLE

> *There is nothing more exciting for me than when someone in the audience "gets it!" A transfer from me to them and back to me.*
>
> Yo Yo Ma

- The speaker sets the dial and spins the energy wheel.
- The audience picks up the frequency and transmits energy back to the speaker.
- The loop is formed!

When speaker and audience get on the same frequency, it's pure pleasure; for those moments alone, we would walk through fire! It's a mutual excitement feed, each connected within the circle of energy, each making the other's game better. If you want to be a speaker of impact, you have to learn how to connect the ends, how to plug yourself into the loop, and how to keep the energy strong. This is a very big subject, but the starting place is with your own energy. You must know how to (1) clear it, (2) direct it, 3) protect it, and (4) connect it.

1. Clear Your Energy

Everything the body can do is potentially enjoyable, if transformed so as to produce flow.

Mihaly Csikszentmihalyi, *Flow*

There are days when everything flows, and there are days when nothing moves! There are speeches that take off and talks that don't make it out of the hangar. With the same presentation you can excite an audience one week and lay an egg the next. What's going on? It's not the weather, and it's not the audience; a good place to look is to the quality of your own energy.

You do not *create* energy, you *are* energy, and that energy has to move; when it's stuck, it produces stale, unproductive emissions. You know this in terms of physical health; maintaining a healthy body is more than the absence of sickness, it's the presence of inner flow. Building a healthy speaking energy is more than not making mistakes, it's that inner aliveness and movement.

When I see speakers, wooden, glued to the floor, stuck in the mechanics of their scripts, bodies locked into a forward lean, and trying so hard to connect with their audiences, I know that the inner flow is stuck. I want to run up on the stage and shout, *Dance*—I mean it, *dance!* Put on some music with a good beat, and give your speech to that beat! Let your body move, free up the shoulders, swivel those hips, get out of your head and get happy; then, bring *that* energy to the audience, and invite them into the dance!" I don't care if you're talking on the mechanics of business writing, if you can't dance with it, it's dead—dead emission. Energy dances, moves, and attracts.

One of the major reasons people say they can't dance is that they are afraid. Fear is the block that stops our energy, fear that we

■ Won't make an impact.
■ Won't give people enough content.
■ Will leave something out.
■ Don't have enough expertise.
■ Will get stumped by an audience question.
■ Won't be taken seriously.
■ Don't have the right approach.
■ Will forget or go blank.
■ Won't get the handouts on time.
■ Don't have an extra bulb for the projector.

Every energy block I can think of is connected to fear.

■ *Trying too hard* connects with the fear that we won't get through to an audience.
■ *Perfectionism* is linked to the fear of losing control.
■ *Indecisiveness* goes to fear of being wrong or unaccepted.

Belief systems of limitation, scarcity, pain, and struggle are all connected to fear, and they shut down movement. People tighten up, breathing gets shallow, and something in them shuts down. You can tell by a person's facial expression and body posture when his or her belief system is around life being tough, pain being necessary, and success being limited. You can feel the results of fear in the pulse of an audience, but you cannot help that audience unless you clear your own energy.

Ways to Clear Your Energy

1. *Release the breath.* Heave a sigh of relief; draw a long deep one.
2. *Loosen up.* Untie, unbuckle, let down your hair.
3. *Suspend judgment.* Ease up, relax it, throw it away, let it be, leave it to God.
4. *Talk it through.* Get it off your chest, put it on the table, talk to yourself.
5. *Make a decision.* Figure it out, look at the big picture, find a way, do it.
6. *Give yourself permission.* Open the door, allow yourself, surrender the struggle.
7. *Acknowledge.* Let someone know, admit it, call it by its name.
8. *Detach.* Cut the cord, turn your back, put some distance between.
9. *Walk away.* Throw it out, get rid of it, recycle, get free.

2. Direct Your Energy

The Single Eye

In the New Testament, it reads that if our eye is single our whole body is full of light. Light and positive energy are companions; both are charged with the power of the single eye.

It's a paradox: We have two eyes, yet we have one. Both eyes work individually, yet we see one image. As it takes the connection of a negative and positive charge to produce light, so it takes both eyes merging into one clarity to open us to light, understanding, knowing, and the release of energy. Direct your energy first to the power of your single eye; find your focus.

Focus

I know a man who likes his wife to drive when they are on trips so that he can shoot pictures from the passenger window. At the end of the trip, his wife sifts through hundreds of unidentifiable shots of freeways, fields, and fuzz. He likes to click the clicker but has no context, no focus from which to shoot.

Speakers can have a similar problem: There is so much out there to shoot, it's tough to choose, so maybe—a little of everything. I hear speakers say,

- "My training is in communication, but I'm developing a talk on change, since it's a hot topic."
- "My focus is on team building, creativity, the future, performance improvement, and time management."

Sure, and I bet you have a lot of fuzzy pictures! The farther back you stand to get everything in, the more you lose detail and wind up with a nice picture of nothing special. Your focus, as a speaker, is the zoom in your camera lens, the merging into the single eye. It's the part of the big picture that you consciously select, narrow, and give passion to. Whatever it takes for you to get to the single eye, once you commit to it, you stop dividing your energies, and you start to build the power for liftoff.

Commitment

An airplane directs all its fuel and power in the flight of a specific route. Passengers board, hatch doors close, and the huge body laboriously moves out onto the runway. Although it may sit on that runway for hours, slowly inching ahead, when the time comes for takeoff, the plane stops, gives full power to its engines, produces one tremendous blast, and lifts! This is commitment. If you want to fly with an audience, forgo the other possible routes, and put everything on the one that will carry you. There's a passage from Goethe that has helped me with this kind of commitment, helped me to trust the single eye:

The moment one definitely commits oneself
Then providence moves too.
All sorts of things occur to help
That would never otherwise have occurred.
A whole stream of events issue from the decision
Rising in one's favor
All manner of unforeseen incidents and
meetings and material assistance
Which no man could have dreamt
would have come his way.

3. Protect Your Energy

Angry and disturbed energies are all around us: the tailgater
on the freeway, the person who pushes ahead of you in the
grocery line, the put-down from a dissatisfied customer,
inner-city kids who terrorize bus passengers, the person
shouting to no one in the middle of the street, the supervisor
who lays his own stress onto loyal workers, and so on. We
have to be constantly on our guard lest these energies creep
into us and perniciously take root.

Sometimes speakers talk about energy suckers, wipeouts,
and tough takes—the difficult audiences—the ones that they
stagger away from, drained. I want to say something here
about the "difficult people" syndrome that has been pro-
moted in books and seminars over the last 20 years. The linear, thinker part of me says that there are no difficult people,
just difficult behaviors; the doer, experiencer part of me says,
"I don't care what you call them, some people are difficult!"
And it's "yes" to both, because no matter what words we use,
we are the ones who have a difficult time and feel the energy
drain. It may relieve our stress to label them "difficult audiences," but we need to take a closer look at what is really
going on. What is it that really drains our energy? Let's look
at four sources for energy drain with audiences:

1. *The negative drain.* Negative means to negate: to refuse, to disagree, to contradict, to oppose, to disprove. An audience that's into negation on some level blocks movement. Sometimes it's just the absence of the positive or a lack of constructive comments that drain us; we walk away feeling ineffective from the absence of any validating response. When people are unhappy, dissatisfied, or fearful, there's a good chance that they are putting out some negative energy that can easily affect the speaker. Employees who are feeling pressured and unacknowledged, care-givers who are exhausted and into overload, service people who deal with the throwaway abuses from the public—all are likely to send out some contagious negative germs, and the speaker can't afford to get them. With some audiences, we have to take precautions.

2. *The hostile drain.* You can feel the difference between negative and hostile: negative grumbles, complains, and whines; hostile attacks or withdraws. With negative you have to protect yourself from leakage onto you; with hostile, you have to stop the urge to defend yourself.

Hostile audiences will confront, call you on a specific point, present evidence that counters what you are saying, make you wrong in front of the group, and put you down. Hostile audiences will also give you the stone-cold silent treatment—no comments, no questions, they do the minimum, and they turn off! The challenge here is to break through the hostility block without putting yourself on the defensive. This takes conscious discipline and the decision not to go on the defensive.

3. *The dead drain.* Some audiences are not just turned off, they're not connected up to any power. These audiences may have nice shining faces and sit in their places, they may even smile, but you can't find anyone home! It's like talking to mannequins: You leave exhausted from trying to find a power socket. The challenge with the dead is to stay alive and not to stay long.

4. *The toxic drain.* This is sometimes the toughest to recognize because we keep thinking that maybe the reason we feel so crummy in their presence is *us.* They may be nice people, not negative or hostile, but like a cancer that quietly eats up all your cells, you not only feel wiped out but a little sick when you're with them. Have you ever been around people who make you physically ill? Whatever is going on, your body reacts, and you know when you're with toxic energies by the way you feel when you're around them. If you have these responses around certain audiences, recognize this, and if it happens more than once, walk away. The world is large, and there are plenty of wonderful people to interact with; why fight it! The challenge here is to recognize and accept what's happening, to not take it personally or judgmentally, just to move on.

Your Best Protection

Your best protection against these drains is to keep your own energy strong. As with your physical health, you pick up toxic energies when your resistance is low. It takes constant attention to your physical and emotional health and the decision to keep your own needs replenished. When you keep excitement and joy alive in your speaking, your energy field stays clear and powerful.

Wherever there is output, there has to be input. Using the analogy of the light bulb, we can change the output by how much of the available energy we use, but the supply, the current and volts, remains the same. If we, however, plug in more and more bulbs, we eventually blow the fuses. As speakers, we have to be careful not to blow our fuses. The law of perpetual motion says that whatever energy we spend, we must regenerate. When we give energy out, we have to recharge. Letting our energy run down to empty lowers our resistance and leaves us vulnerable.

- Learn to recognize when you're up against an energy drain.
- Speak to groups that help you recharge.
- Stay out of situations that put you into recovery.
- Don't try so hard that you give away your energy.
- Stay away from the drainers.
- Keep with the single eye; keep reconnecting with your focus.

Probably your best protection is to keep radiating energy yourself. Use it, don't lose it; don't hold back on your capacities to be spontaneous and joyful. Stop comparing yourself with others and their ability to give a "better talk." The late, great American trumpet player Dizzy Gillespie once revealed in an interview that he never looked behind him to find out what the other person was playing or doing. He said, "I just keep going, looking for new ideas, practicing, and playing my horn." Do what you love for the sake of expressing your aliveness. Forget it, if someone doesn't like it; just keep it flowing. This is the best guarantee for a healthy body and a vibrant presentation energy.

4. Connect Your Energies

Hook into the power of the collective energy.

The organist touches a chord on the cathedral keyboard, and the heavens open! The conductor flicks one finger, and a whole orchestra responds! We have not begun to tap the power of the collective energy; what can 100 people produce, each focused on a single thought at a single time?

American country and western singer Naomi Judd used her audiences to physically heal herself. Dying with hepatitis C, an incurable liver disease, she booked an extensive farewell performance tour that to many seemed impossible. But to her, she was not saying goodbye, she was consciously healing herself with the love and applause of the audiences. We're dabbling with powerful mixes, explosives that hold great power.

In 1998 the Space Telescope Science Institute of Baltimore, Maryland, and the University of California at Los Angeles, California, announced a newly found star, brighter than ten million suns. An image was captured by the Hubble telescope that showed the most powerful star ever observed, surrounded by a cloud, or nebula, produced by violent eruptions on its surface.

Upon reading this, I thought, "Wow! That's us!" On one hand, our power for brightness is inexhaustible; on the other, we spend a lot of time in a fog because of the eruptions on our surface. Astronomers tell us that in many ways, we know less about the center of our own galaxy than we do about the center of other and more distant galaxies.

This book has been a study first of our own galaxy—our center—and then a guide for bringing the more distant audience galaxies in closer so we can connect with our whole universe.

Impact is connection.
It is not sought nor crafted.
Though it is not applause,
It is the touch of two hands.
Impact is who we are,
What we bring to the table,
How we care and
How we serve
Ourselves and our audiences.
Impact is when
Love connects.

About Toastmasters International

If the thought of public speaking is enough to stop you dead in your tracks, it may have the same effect on your career.

While surveys report that public speaking is one of people's most dreaded fears, the fact remains that the inability to effectively deliver a clear thought in front of others can spell doom for professional progress. The person with strong communication skills has a clear advantage over tongue-tied colleagues—especially in a competitive job market.

Toastmasters International, a nonprofit educational organization, helps people conquer their pre-speech jitters. From one club started in Santa Ana, California, in 1924, the organization now has more than 170,000 members in 8,300 clubs in 62 countries.

How Does It Work?

A Toastmasters club is a "learn by doing" workshop in which men and women hone their communication and leadership skills in a friendly, supportive atmosphere. A typical club has 20 members who meet weekly or biweekly to practice public speaking techniques. Members, who pay approximately $35 in dues twice a year, learn by progressing through a series of 10 speaking assignments and being evaluated on their performance by their fellow club members. When finished with the basic speech manual, members can select from among 14 advanced programs that are geared toward specific career needs. Members also have the opportunity to develop and practice leadership skills by working in the High Performance Leadership Program.

Besides taking turns to deliver prepared speeches and evaluate those of other members, Toastmasters give impromptu talks on assigned topics, usually related to current events. They also develop listening skills, conduct meetings, learn parliamentary procedure and gain leadership experience by serving as club officers. But most importantly, they develop self-confidence from accomplishing what many once thought impossible.

The benefits of Toastmasters' proven and simple learning formula has not been lost on the thousands of corporations that sponsor in-house Toastmasters clubs as cost-efficient means of satisfying their employees' needs for communication training. Toastmasters clubs can be found in the U.S. Senate and the House of Representatives, as well as in a variety of community organizations, prisons, universities, hospitals, military bases, and churches.

How to Get Started

Most cities in North America have several Toastmasters clubs that meet at different times and locations during the week. If you are interested in forming or joining a club, call (714) 858-8255. For a listing of local clubs, call (800) WE-SPEAK, or write Toastmasters International, PO Box 9052, Mission Viejo, California 92690, USA. You can also visit our website at http://www.toastmasters.org.

As the leading organization devoted to teaching public speaking skills, we are devoted to helping you become more effective in your career and daily life.

Terrence J. McCann
Executive Director, Toastmasters International

Allyn & Bacon Order Form
The Essence of Public Speaking series

NOW YOU CAN ORDER THE REST OF THE BOOKS IN THE SERIES!

New Books in the Series!

☐ *Speaking for Impact,* by Shirley E. Nice,
Order # T7025-4, $14.95

☐ *Choosing Powerful Words,* by Ronald H. Carpenter,
Order # T7124-5, $14.95

☐ *Delivering Dynamic Presentations,* by Ralph Hillman,
Order # T6810-0, $14.95

☐ *Involving Your Audience,* by Karen Lawson,
Order # T6811-8, $14.95

☐ *Motivating Your Audience,* by Hanoch McCarty,
Order # T6894-4, $14.95

Previously Published Titles in the Series

☐ *Speaking for Profit and Pleasure,* by William D. Thompson,
Order # T7026-2, $12.00

☐ *Speaking Your Way to the Top,* by Marjorie Brody,
Order # T6814-2, $12.00

☐ *TechEdge,* by William J. Ringle,
Order # T7305-0, $12.00

☐ *Using Stories and Humor,* by Joanna Slan,
Order # T6893-6, $12.00

☐ *Writing Great Speeches,* by Alan Perlman,
Order # T7300-1, $12.00

Name: _____

Address: _____

City: _____ State: _____ Zip:_____

Phone: _____ E-mail: _____

__Charge my   __AMEX   __VISA   __Mastercard   __Discover

Credit Card # _____ Exp. Date _____

MPG002   B1270A2-9

To place an order:

MAIL:
Allyn & Bacon Publishers
111 10th Street
Des Moines, IA 50309

CALL toll-free: 1-800-278-3525
FAX: 1-515-284-2607
WEBSITE: www.abacon.com